LOVING
A PRODIGAL

LOVING A PRODIGAL

A Survival Guide
for Parents of Rebellious Children

H. NORMAN WRIGHT

Chariot Victor Publishing
A Division of Cook Communications

Chariot Victor Publishing
A division of Cook Communications, Colorado Springs, Colorado 80918
Cook Communications, Paris, Ontario, Canada
Kingsway Communications, Eastbourne, England

Cover and Interior Design: Image Studios

1 2 3 4 5 6 7 8 9 10 Printing/Year 03 02 01 00 99

Library of Congress Cataloging-in-Publication Data

Wright, H. Norman.
　　Loving a prodigal/by H. Norman Wright.
　　　　p.　　cm.
　　Includes bibliographical references.
　　ISBN 1-56476-743-4
　　1. Problem children.　　2. Problem youth.　　3. Parenting.　　I. Title.
HQ773.W75　　1999　　　　　　　　　　　　　　99-21017
649'.64--dc21　　　　　　　　　　　　　　　　　CIP

Table of Contents

If you know people who have
wandered off from God's truth,
don't write them off.

Go after them.

Get them back and you will have
rescued precious lives from destruction
and prevented an epidemic of
wandering away from God.

James 5:19-20,
The Message

CHAPTER ONE

You Have a Prodigal

I t often begins with a phone call. It may be from a police officer, teacher, pastor, friend, newspaper reporter, or even from your son or daughter. Whoever it is, they are telling you something you never wanted to hear, something that causes you to go weak with shock, disbelief, and dismay.

"Mom, Dad, I'm gay."

"I'm pregnant."

"I'm living with my girlfriend."

"Your son has been arrested for selling coke."

"I'm moving out. I can't stand the restrictions here."

"I'm dropping out of school. It's a waste, and I won't graduate anyway."

"Your daughter is in the hospital. She tried to take her life."

"I have AIDS."

Such words shake the very foundations of a home and family. Everything you've worked for, prayed for, and sacrificed for has just crumbled.

It may be that the awareness of a problem came more gradually, like a hairline crack you can't seem to patch spreading an inch at a time on the face of a dam, until finally the dam breaks and the water comes rushing in. Either way, the impact is so strong it numbs you, and then emotions rage. One moment the sky of your life is clear. The next, you feel as though you're caught up in a tornado.

Storms are like that. They often appear out of nowhere at the wrong time. They're not just inconvenient; they're destructive. For some, life is never the same afterwards.

Storms come in all kinds and intensities. In your life, the storm may be a dramatic one—a child running away, getting involved in drugs or alcohol, being sexually promiscuous, joining a cult, changing his or her sexual orientation, or a host of other behaviors. Or your cause for concern may be more like a slow, steady rain, eroding the foundation you have so carefully laid for your child's life—a persistent lack of effort at school, no desire to attend church functions, a preference for deadbeat friends. Either way, the result is the same—inside, you feel shattered. Listen to a few of the many parents of prodigals that I interviewed as I researched this book:

> And your struggles and pain intensify each day. Your response is likely similar to the response of other parents who have been in your shoes: My immediate reaction was to blank out. My emotions were blocked off and numbed due to shock. . . . I blamed myself for failing as a parent. What did I do wrong? I blamed my husband for not being involved in family relationships. . . . I also felt total helplessness. I didn't have the maturity to go to church for help and support. I felt ashamed and hid from other friends, who didn't have my problem. I was closed in. My family fought a lot and I cried a lot.

> Our immediate reaction was heartache, crying and feeling as if we should wear some or all of the guilt. I particularly wore a lot of guilt for anything we might have done to alienate [our daughter] from the primary focus of Christianity in our home. I might add we have faithfully (I mean faithfully) tithed, gone to church (not church-hopped), served in our church, prayed, read our Bible daily, been faithful to each other, been consistent with our faith her entire life. But there are still times where we let her down, I'm sure, and I recently at least had the chance to ask her to forgive us for any times that might have hurt her.

> When I first heard him utter the words, "For the past four years I've been living a gay lifestyle, I felt numb, sick to my stomach, and felt like I wanted to be anywhere but where I was. I tried to

talk "sense" to him, but it was clear he wasn't interested in anything I had to say. After the initial upheaval of the revelation, I did find myself reliving the past eighteen years of his life and asking myself, "Where did I miss the signs?" "What did I do wrong?" At first I couldn't understand how this could be happening since I had raised all my children in the same way, with the same standards, values, etc.—all the things that were so important to me—and one had strayed so far from the path!

It's like a roller coaster. First, I felt shock and disbelief. Then a terrible amount of guilt, followed by wanting to figure out how to fix the problem. Next, to release the problem and realize that it's a problem for my son to solve. I'm available to my son for love and support. My son would improve for awhile—then there would be another phone call from the police. The emotional roller coaster would start all over again.

You're a hurting parent. Buddy Scott describes well why you hurt:

You hurt . . .
because the children you love have turned toward self-destruction.
because your children stand in grotesque defiance against you.

because your megacontribution to the lives of your kids is not being appreciated by them.

You hurt . . .
because you feel like failures as parents.

because you are haunted by your thoughts, *If only we had done this or done that.*

because other parents—some with younger children or some fortunate enough not to have had severe problems with their teenagers—look at you like you are failures.

because you are frustrated from going behind your kids cleaning up their messes.

because you have to mix with people at work, at community functions, or at church who know about your children's problems.

because you wonder if you ought to give up your positions at church or in the community.

You hurt . . .
because you don't know for sure how to help your children.

because you don't know what to do or how to think.[1]

Our many joyful experiences with our children produce a reservoir of fond memories. I often reflect on them, as you probably do. Remember those first days of school when your child came racing home to share his or her exciting discoveries? I do. I also remember watching our five-year-old daughter bait her own hook with a live anchovy on a deep-sea fishing boat, toss the bait into the water, and reel in her fish all by herself. That trip led to many experiences of hiking and boating with her throughout Montana and Wyoming.

I think of her final piano recital when she was in high school. She talked me into playing a duet with her for her last number. It was supposed to be a serious recital, but we soon destroyed that image. As we played, the music slid off the piano into our laps, and we couldn't stop laughing until we concluded the piece. I'm glad that happened, because the event is much more vivid in my memory than it would have been otherwise.

I also remember listening to Sheryl describe how she had invited Jesus Christ into her life and the joy I experienced over that. Perhaps you've had that experience with your child as well.

But entwined with those memories are the dreams you had for your child's future. When she tended that wounded bird, you wondered, "Will she be a veterinarian?" When he hit that home run, you thought, "Maybe he'll be an athlete!" Playing dress-up and house made you envision a wedding day and grandchildren; good report cards conjured up images of doctors' scrubs or suits and ties. Perhaps most poignant were the moments when your child's voice rang out pure and high in the singing of a hymn or the praying of a prayer, and you saw his or her future as a committed child of God.

Every parent dreams about the future. The dreams may change from time to time as the parents become more aware of the unique qualities and characteristics of their child. But the dreams remain, continuing to involve the best for the child. The dreams usually include the child developing talents to the fullest, reflecting the parents' Christian values, perhaps accomplishing what other parents' children are unable to, and even fulfilling some of the unfulfilled dreams the parents had for themselves. But right now it may seem that those dreams are turning to dust, right before their eyes.

A prodigal. Not a pleasant term. It leaves a bad taste in your mouth and a sinking feeling in the pit of your stomach. It's a label given to people who are wasteful. But it's not just money they waste. It's the value system you've been trying to instill. It's their potential, their abilities, their health, perhaps even their lives. It's upsetting to you, but in many cases, they really don't care. When a child—whether a teen or an adult—becomes a prodigal, dreams are tarnished. Sometimes they're not just damaged, they're shattered. Some are kept faintly alive like the smoldering coals of a fire; others die. It's difficult to say which is hardest.

One writer offers us an insightful perspective on this particular subject:

> Many parents see their children as extensions of themselves, or as their possessions, or as the fulfillment of their unfulfilled lives. These are all potentially destructive attitudes to have toward raising one's children. All of these "beliefs" make children into "little idols" in one form or another. We "idolize" them. We hallow them and their achievements. We have to, because we have invested so much of ourselves in them. Such idolatry, created by unresolved grief, not only blocks grieving, but blocks the opportunity to discover our children as adults.
>
> The central theological question is: "Whom do our children belong to?" For people of faith, the answer should be: God. Isn't that what we acknowledge in infant baptism or dedication? God gives them to us as gifts. They are on loan. Our job is to raise them, teach them, love them and then launch them into the world, thereby returning them to God. They are with us only for a short time.[2]

When a dream is damaged or has died, it, like any other loss in life, must be grieved over before you can move on. Some parents create greater pain for themselves by failing to say good-bye to a dead or damaged dream. They keep trying to resurrect their original dream. They attempt to breathe new life into it, like giving CPR to a corpse. When a dream cannot be fulfilled or is mortally wounded, the only alternative is to create new dreams. This is what parents who survive the years of their child's wandering have learned to do in order to survive as well as to resurrect hope.

> I've dreamed many dreams that never came true
> I've seen them vanish at dawn,
> But I've realized enough of my dreams, thank God
> *To make me want to dream on.*

> I've prayed many prayers when no answer came,
> Though I waited patient and long,
> But answers have come to enough of my prayers
> *To make me keep praying on.*

> I've trusted many a friend who failed
> And left me to weep alone;
> But I've found enough of my friends true blue
> *To make me keep trusting on.*

> I've sown many seeds that fell by the way
> For the birds to feed upon,
> But I've held enough golden sheaves in my hands
> *To make me keep sowing on.*

> I've drained the cup of disappointment and pain
> And gone many days without song;
> But I've sipped enough nectar from the roses of life
> *To make me want to live on.*

> —Author Unknown

As willing as you may be to move on, the death of those dreams in which you have been so invested leaves you feeling abused and victimized. As one parent said, "I feel like I'm going through a divorce, not by my spouse but by my seventeen-year-old. Our relationship has crumbled. He won't even talk to us anymore, let alone listen to any suggestions or even help. And I've pretty well planned on burying all my hopes for him going to that Christian college. He won't go to church anymore. He told me that he doesn't even believe anymore. Maybe I ought to have a funeral service for the future! It sure looks dead to me!"

Your prodigal's choices also end up controlling your life to some extent. It's a struggle for every family, as these parents share.

I tried to keep my homosexual son's actions from controlling my life, but at first it was difficult because the pain and loss were so great. I wanted to be available if he called, so I wanted to be home a lot. Then when I was out, I remember thinking, "If these people only knew the pain I'm in," or sometimes I just wanted to shout out my grief to the world! My spouse wanted to move on with our life more than I wanted to and he was the one who suggested the house rearranging—I would have left [my son's] room as it was for a little longer, till I worked through a bit more of my grief. But in retrospect I think it was the best thing to do because it kept me busy.

What our daughter did totally controlled our life. After my marriage broke up (not at all because of my daughter) my daughter lived with my mom and me. She then got pregnant, had the baby, and immediately started hanging out, doing drugs and staying out every night. Actually it started about ten months after my grandson was born. She was only sixteen or seventeen years old and not at all ready to be a mom. Because of my grandson I put up with much more than I should have for fear she would try to take him out of my home. There was a lot of manipulation and control on her part because she knew I loved my grandson and wanted a safe home for him. Her behavior controlled all of our lives at the time.

Often I made poor choices to get on with life by filling the time with meaningless activity such as cleaning the already clean house or shopping for unnecessary "things." For months I realized I was out of control, allowing pain to affect a lot of my decisions. If I was discouraged, I blamed my son, if I was sleepless it was because I was thinking or praying about my son. . . . Although he was miles away, my moods and reactions were . . . colored by the memory of his words that I believed were cruel and unjustified. Temporary victory came when I heeded the faithful support from my prayer partner and husband who pointed me back to reality and helped me to get a grip on life. I must confess this was a battleground for me to try to remain stable, and not be disabled by depression and evasion of the issues by becoming exhausted.

Right now I feel that she in many ways is controlling our lives. We are all functioning in dissonance. Our ten-year-old is greatly affected. When the prodigal is around, tensions run high and he exhibits acting-out behaviors.

In some aspects our daughter's actions certainly controlled our family's life. Vacations were tough. We literally could not trust her to be by herself; whenever we did probably 80 percent of the time we caught her in lies/bad activities—so if she wasn't with us we were concerned. After a while you understand you can only do so much, and I basically said whatever she chooses to do, she'll do, and worrying about it just won't help. We talked openly with her sisters, if they felt like it—but they didn't want to say much. I did not realize just how much our youngest was affected—I think it was significant, but I still don't know why.

The author of *Surviving the Prodigal Years* describes the widespread impact of a prodigal's behavior:

As the pain of the prodigal years increases, we find we are deal-ing with more than just our personal sense of guilt. As the load escalates, it sucks in other people. Both parents, whether they are currently married to each other or not, are snagged and flung into the angry sea of emotions. Siblings, the extended family, and friends are snared and left floundering, unrestrained for the shock of torn relationships.

The strain on the fabric of families can cause frayed edges and unraveled seams. We are so interwoven with one another that when one person rips away from the others, the continuity and strength of the family can be severely damaged.

We all react in our own way. Some withdraw, some turn to a friend, some become more untied. People need to be extremely sensitive to the feelings, emotions, and pain of the people around them. The prodigal years can cause parents and families to bond more tightly or to be ripped apart. . . .

It can be easy to slip into depression, individually, as a couple, or even as a whole family. Having a prodigal child is very much like experiencing a death in the family. In fact, it is a type of death—the termination of family life as it was known.[3]

You may feel a bit intimidated because you're not sure what to do, either about your prodigal or about his or her impact on the rest of your family. You may also feel intimidated because you don't agree with your partner on what to do.

Perhaps the scariest intimidation is the risk involved in demanding appropriate behavior. You may be afraid that your action might cause your children to:

run away

drop out of school

fail to graduate from high school and college

lose their jobs

talk against you to significant others

report you to child welfare for child abuse

turn further away from you and toward the wrong crowd

get deeper into drugs

get someone pregnant or get pregnant

and so forth

Defiant and rebellious kids become aware of your dreadful anxieties and use them against you. *They will sometimes grab hold of your fears and use them as tools of manipulation to further intimidate you. They threaten to make your worst fears come true if you continue to interfere in their lives.* You may be left shivering in swamps of despair.

Abused parents can be benched by the anxieties that spew from in*timid*ation.

Abused parents are often benched by anxiety attacks. You sometimes sit with your head in your hands bewildered about what to do. You feel powerless, confused, and guilty.

It's as if you have become an *invalid* parent. Just think of what the word *invalid* means: "having become incapable of caring for oneself, sick." Another meaning of *invalid* is "nonvalid, not worth anything."[4]

You do feel immobilized. We know. We felt that way during the first few months our daughter was away from the Lord. You feel torn between wanting to do something that will work and not wanting to do anything that will make the situation worse. You may feel left in the dark, not even knowing what's going on with your child. Part of you wants all the details, and part of you is afraid of hearing the worst. In one way we were fortunate, because the lines of communication between Sheryl and us were never cut off. We usually knew what was going on, but sometimes that intensified our pain, because it heightened our feelings of helplessness.

One of my most difficult tasks as a father and husband was having to tell Joyce what was occurring with our daughter. Sheryl had made an appointment to see me at the end of my office hours one day, but I didn't know that until I went out to the desk and glanced at my appointment book. I was surprised to see Sheryl's name written in it. I went back into my office, and she was sitting there quietly, waiting for me.

I was puzzled about why she was there, and for the first few minutes, nothing significant seemed to transpire. But then she said, "The reason I'm here, Daddy, is that I've never lied to you and Mother before, and I'm not going to now. I wanted to let you and Mother know that I'm living with my boyfriend."

We continued to talk calmly. I told her I appreciated her telling me directly so I wouldn't hear about it from someone else. But already a sense of weight and dread was creeping through my emotions.

We parted, and I went outside, got in my car, and just sat there for a moment. Numbness from the shock settled in as I drove home. I relived the conversation a dozen times or more. Perhaps part of the reason I went through it so many times had to do with hope. I was hoping I would discover that it was all a bad dream, that it hadn't happened and wasn't true. And by rehashing it again and again, I was probably delaying what I knew was inevitable—having to tell Joyce.

I started to formulate and rehearse what I was going to say to her. I wanted to postpone or avoid it. I didn't want to inflict what I knew would be an incredible amount of pain on her. But I couldn't escape the inevitable. When I finally broke the news, I could see the impact it had on her, and I wished again that it weren't true and that I didn't have to be the one to tell her.

Joyce's response, though, was different from what I had anticipated. The news confirmed where she felt Sheryl's path had been leading. Rather than being stunned, Joyce was hurt and sad, because she knew such a lifestyle wouldn't bring Sheryl happiness. Joyce also realized Sheryl had made a conscious decision to step out of God's will, so she began to firmly pray against that choice.

For the next four years, we felt as though we were in an emotional Death Valley. It was the most difficult time in our parenting role apart from the time, two years earlier, when we placed our retarded son, Matthew, in a home for the disabled. We seemed to go from one crisis to another. We experienced situations that we had heard of in the lives of other families but had never anticipated occurring in our own.

Who would have thought that one of Sheryl's fiancés would turn out to be a drug dealer and physical abuser? Or that she would have to move home because of a difficult situation with a roommate who was dealing drugs? At least that time we were able to take some action by reporting the person to the authorities.

Seldom did we have an opportunity to feel any sense of control. Despite the pain, we spent many enjoyable hours with Sheryl that gave us hope for our relationship. But overall it was a time of sadness, because we saw no indication that she might reverse her course of action. We were often tempted to point out the pitfalls of what she was doing and correct her. Most of the time we kept quiet, however, because our mentioning the situation only aroused her defensiveness. And then we learned that she was already struggling under a load of guilt and certainly didn't need more.

Of course, knowing how to handle an offending child is not easy. John Hinckley, for instance, who attempted to assassinate President Reagan, was a prodigal. His parents had tried various steps and treatments to help their drifting, failure-oriented child to attend school, work, live on his own, and become self-sufficient. A psychologist advised them to use a "tough love" approach and turn him out of their home. But what this son needed rather than a tough love approach was hospitalization and treatment. He didn't need to be cut off from his parents' help. He was struggling with the distorted thinking pattern of schizophrenia, not willful disobedience. The story could have ended very differently had his parents discovered this earlier.

There are times when it's difficult to distinguish between mental problems and rebellion and thus know how to respond. I've seen older adolescents create chaos in their home because of their bizarre and impulsive behavior, only to finally discover that they are bipolar (have a manic-depressive disorder). The solution is treatment and medication rather then discipline or a tough love approach. But sometimes mental problems are not discovered until there is an episode or a breakdown.[5] If you are there, you know the self-recriminations are endless.

Having a child rebel is difficult for any parent, but a different dynamic enters the picture when the child is an adult and the parents are older. The relationship has changed from parent-child to a more adult-to-adult connection. There is more of a peerlike relationship.

Of all rebellions, that of an adult child is possibly the most distressing and long-lasting. With teenagers, you're always holding your breath, waiting for something to happen. But who expects a child of thirty or forty to throw away his values and embrace those he formerly took a stand against?

When the adult child makes a major change in his life—such as leaving his spouse for another, proclaiming she's gay, being arrested for embezzlement or involvement with drugs, becoming an alcoholic, or physically or sexually abusing his children, etc.—the hopes and dreams that the parents have come to consider reality are shattered. The parents have by now relaxed their role as parents. They were able to get their child through the perils of adolescence and have let their guard down. But then the news hits them. It's a crisis. It's a loss. And it's likely that they are now dealing with their own developmental losses as well. They may be seeing the top of their vocational ladder or be facing joblessness due to "downscaling"; they may be in the process of relocating, facing health problems, or caring for aging parents; they may be starting to lose their contemporaries to death or illness, may even have lost their own spouse through death or divorce. With everything else occurring in their lives, difficulty with an adult child robs them of a source of their satisfaction. The way in which they talk about this child will change. Instead of volunteering information about her, they may be vague or hesitant to talk. If this child was well known or even famous, what the parents were known for has now been shattered and some social status is gone.

If the parents were dependent upon their adult child in any way, they may feel torn between their need to stay dependent, if they're able to do so, and wonder whether or not it's all right. They may be called on to help in some way that could tax their resources, cripple their retirement or travel plans, or impact their living arrangements.

There is another unique problem that arises. If the adult child was married and had a family, much of the support and concern will be directed toward the spouse and grandchildren rather than the parents. It's as though you're experiencing a major loss or crisis in your life that isn't legitimized by society. You feel as though you're on your own. When you share the situation with others, instead of receiving the empathetic and caring responses yourself, you hear, "Oh, that poor wife and those little children. How could he do that to them?" And you want to shout, "But what about us!"

In time, if the problem was an affair and/or divorce, the parents could lose contact with the grandchildren. They may have reservations about the new stepparent as well.

Regardless of the prodigal's age, one of the most devastating experiences is when the consequences of a prodigal's choices can't be reversed. The young teen who becomes pregnant is now a mother whether she keeps the baby or not. If she gives the baby up, she will grieve its loss. If she aborts the child, she carries the emotional wounds throughout her life. And unless she asks the Lord's forgiveness, which can fully cleanse her, she will always have that ache. Years of drug or alcohol abuse tear down the body's organs and tissues, and some never recover. And, tragically, both heterosexual and homosexual experiences can lead to the ultimate disease of the twentieth century, AIDS. Besides the physical consequences, there will be those who shun this child because of their fear of contracting the disease.

Where do you go from here? You'd probably like to get out of the storm that's disrupting your life. But like a rainstorm or a blizzard, there's no real way to know when this storm will end. Storms are a part of nature. They're also part of our lives. There is hope, however. I once heard someone say, "When you're in a thunderstorm, always look for the rainbow."

There were three men in the Bible who saw rainbows. One was Noah, who saw the rainbow *after* the storm. Like him, there will be a day in the future when you'll see a rainbow again. Count on that.

Ezekiel saw the rainbow in the *midst* of the storm. Even though he and the other Jews had been exiled to Babylon and Jerusalem and the temple was about to be destroyed, he knew by the rainbow that God was still there. You can't ignore your storm, but you can look for the rainbow. It's there.

In Revelation we read that John saw the rainbow *before* the storm. He saw a complete circle, not just the bow. It meant that God would be in control before, during, and after the storm he was learning about. Hear these words from a message by a retired missionary who experienced many storms in life:

> You and I will experience storms until we are called to heaven; and then all storms will cease. Expect the storms and don't be afraid of them, because God is always faithful.
>
> Just remember God's message to you: *Always look for the rainbow.* Depend on the faithfulness of God. Sometimes He'll show you the rainbow after the storm, sometimes during the storm, and sometimes before the storm. *But He will never fail you.*[6]

1. Buddy Scott, *Relief for Hurting Parents* (Lake Jackson, Texas: Allon Publishing, 1994) p. 12.
2. R. Scott Sullender, *Losses in Later Life* (New York: Integration Books/Paulist Press, 1989), p. 68.
3. Marcia Mitchell, *Surviving the Prodigal Years* (Lynnwood, Wash.: Emerald Books, 1995), pp. 80, 81.
4. Scott, *Relief for Hurting Parents*, pp. 17-18.
5. Sidney Callahan, *Parents Forever* (New York: Crossroad, 1992), pp. 151-155, adapted.
6. Warren W. Wiersbe, *Preaching and Teaching Within a Generation* (Grand Rapids, Mich.: Baker Book House, 1994), p. 59.

CHAPTER TWO

You're Going Through a Crisis

You open your eyes, but you still can't see clearly. You blink and then blink again. Everything is still hazy, as though you are in a thick fog. There is a sense of unreality in everything around you. You feel as though you have been run over by a three-ton truck or as though someone has slammed you over the head with a two-by-four. What has happened? Are you losing your mind?

You've entered the world of a crisis, brought on by your prodigal. Maybe you saw it coming; you watched the signs of rebellion in your child building for years. Or maybe it came as a shock.

Either way, you feel as though part of your life has been amputated. It's like being in a junkyard where a gigantic machine crushes cars into flattened, nonfunctional pieces of scrap. At the beginning of a crisis you feel crushed, ready to be thrown on the scrap heap.

The Impact Phase

This is the stage of a crisis called the *impact phase*.[1] People vary in the intensity of their response to a crisis, but all of us feel the impact. You know immediately that something drastic has happened. You're stunned, perhaps from that phone call, the knock at the door, a note on a pillow, or a police car stopping outside your house.

The impact phase of most crises is brief, lasting from a few hours to a few days, depending upon the event and the person involved. But with prodigals, the impact phase may linger on and on, especially with such long-term situations as a runaway child or one facing a distant court date. Most of us don't realize that what we're experiencing or feeling is a normal response.

Keep this principle in mind—the more severe the child's difficulty, the greater the impact and the greater the amount of incapacitation and numbness for the parent. Tears might come immediately, or they may pour out much later.

People have described the feeling in many ways. Perhaps you can identify with some of these:

At one point I felt as though the ground was opening beneath me! As if I were to look down and the world was going to swallow me up.

I felt like I was in a free fall. But I didn't have a parachute.

It was a strange sensation. I sort of felt as though the world was somehow less real, like I was disconnected, except of course when it came crashing in on me. It was that kind of alternating experience: Sometimes I was "out of it"; sometimes I was in the middle of it; but I could never get away from it.

One parent said:

Although our adopted son made an open profession of faith in Jesus Christ as his Savior and was baptized by profession of faith at fourteen, he believed God created him to be bisexual. After joining the navy, he married a Christian girl from his hometown. As parents, we did not know of his choice to practice this alternative lifestyle until he called long distance with the revelation that he had been released from the pain of severe headaches when he came to grips with his suppression as a person. He called to inform us that he had been "gay" since the day he was born and God had allowed him to be sexually controlled by the male neighbor from the time he was five years old until he was twelve to introduce him to homosexual experiences. Any problems we might have with this declaration were ours to deal with the best way we could.

We both thought there was some mistake in what we were hearing or perhaps we were misunderstanding the terms our son was throwing around like obscene graffiti splattering all over our hearts. Shock registered high on the list of emotions, surfacing right on the heels of denial. As his mother, I questioned why we had endured the pain of adopting a child with fetal alcohol syndrome only to watch all our efforts to provide a stable environment be rejected. It was much easier to take some credit for our son being an officer and a gentleman than it was to take responsibility and acknowledge that he was coming out of the closet and telling our family and friends that he was leading an alternative lifestyle. Embarrassed by this confession, I wanted to retreat from church and become an undercover agent: stay home and hide in bed until he came to his senses.

To Fight or Flee?

During this first phase, one of the questions you must answer is "Should I stay and face the problem, or withdraw and run from it?" This is called the fight or flight instinct. Some parents try to deny the problem: "It's not as bad as they say," or "It will go away on its own," or "They're mistaken. It couldn't have been our son!" Others, though, want to take action immediately without sufficient information or facts. A few years ago, a popular television commercial featured the slogan, "I'd rather fight than switch." But not everyone feels that way in a crisis. If your tendency in the past has been to face problems head-on, you will probably face this crisis head-on. But if your tendency has been to avoid or withdraw from problems, you will probably run from this or the next crisis with your child. If the crisis is especially overwhelming, you may feel like running away, since during this impact phase you're not able to cope as well as you usually do.

Facing a family crisis and fighting to regain control seems to be the healthier response. Most of the time, running from any crisis is not a solution, since it merely prolongs the situation. How can you run from what's happening with your child? And since there are three more phases yet to come before balance is restored, why linger here? Why prolong the pain?

I'm in a Fog!

During this impact stage, don't expect your thinking to be clear. You'll feel numb and disoriented. You may even feel as though you can't think or feel at all. One parent said she felt "as though my entire system shut down." You want to do something about your child, but you're immobilized. Your capacity to be insightful and sharp is limited. Don't expect to have that ability now. If a friend or family member attempts to share any factual information with you, it will probably go sailing right over your head. You may ask, "What did you say?" after it's been repeated for the third time. This response is completely normal.

Keep in mind that your judgment at this time may not be as good as usual. Unfortunately, you may need to make some decisions anyway. Be sure to ask a competent friend to help you.

Dealing with Loss

At the heart of most crises is a loss of some kind. It could be the dreams you had for your child, or your hopes for his or her future, or your own retirement or travel plans. You could even lose contact with your child. Any loss threatens your security, your sense of stability, and your well-being. Your self-image may be affected, and there is the feeling of being out of control. The more sudden the situation with your child, the more out of control you will feel. An unexpected upset may disrupt your ability to activate the emotional resources you need in order to cope.

One of the most difficult types of losses to deal with is the threatened loss. For some, it's like a crisis waiting to happen—the loss hasn't occurred yet, but there is a real possibility that it will. Your child's threat to run away, the wait for the outcome of an AIDS or pregnancy test, or an impending jail sentence puts you in this position.

Any kind of a loss has a way of changing our lives in a dramatic way. Even our thinking about the future is affected. The changes that a crisis brings about can be positive and eventually enrich our lives. But during the first few months of a crisis, it doesn't feel that way to us at all.

If someone were to tell you at the time of a loss that you can learn and grow as you experience this, you might react with disgust or anger. You're not ready to handle thoughts like that. You need to hear such comments, true as they are, when life is fairly stable.

During the impact phase, in one way or another, you'll begin to search for what you've lost. It is normal to search for something that meant a great deal to you, such as a responsive, loving, or obedient child. You are trying to hold onto your emotional attachments for a bit longer. You are trying to recapture the lost dream, the child the way he or she was, or your life the way it was. The more insight you have at this time, the less you'll search, and the less insight, the more you'll search!

This searching behavior often takes on the form of reminiscing. How much you reminisce is in proportion to the value of what you lost. You may find yourself looking through photo albums of happier times, your child's yearbook, or trophies he had accumulated. You may find yourself beginning many conversations with "Remember when . . . ." That's okay.

Express Your Feelings

It's normal and it's also healthy to express as many feelings as you can. You will need someone to listen to you and accept those feelings. *Avoid* those people who try to make you stifle your feelings. Feelings should not be buried or denied at this point, for that will only delay the resolution of the problem. When feelings are buried, they are frozen—not gone.

Do you know what happens to water when it is frozen? The molecules actually expand. Thus water frozen in pipes has the power to burst those steel pipes wide open. Frozen emotions also take on a power out of proportion to their original nature. When we lock up a summer mountain cabin for the winter, it is important to drain all the water from the pipes if we want them to function properly the next spring. During grief and crisis, it is important to keep the channels open so the feelings can flow when they need to.

The feelings you experience in a crisis come as waves. The earthquake intensity of any crisis recedes, and then the tidal waves of emotions begin their hammering process. And they keep rolling in, wave after wave.

These feelings have to have an outlet. If not, they won't stay buried. One day they will explode with a vengeance. One author describes it well:

> I will never forget the time my dad left a can of aerosol spray in the back window of the family car while he was playing golf. The sun pounded on the window for a couple of hours and then the can detonated, shattering the windows and slicing a hole in the steel roof of the car. The force was unimaginable.
>
> It's the same way with unexpressed feelings born in the midst of crisis. They fester and fester until they explode, adding damage to damage, doing nothing to reduce the problem.[2]

Some struggle trying to figure out what they're feeling. Others can't find the words. Look at the illustration of the *Ball of Crisis and Grief* below. Which of these do you identify with?

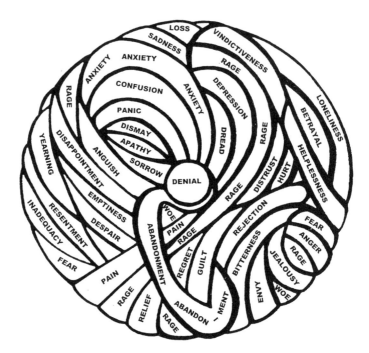

Ball of Crisis and Grief

Some of us release our feelings through verbal expression because that is what we know best. But others find other means to empty themselves of their emotions. We shouldn't compare ourselves with others and say one way of release is the only way or the best way. Some people talk about their hurt and grief and some act it out. One parent may spend a great deal of time working in the yard or running but does not talk about the impact of what her adult daughter did, while another goes over and over the details with anyone who will listen. Each is processing her feelings in her own way.

When the initial shock is over, you begin to feel cheated as well. Not at first, because you're thinking of your child and still wanting the best for him or her. Even in the midst of shock, anger, and outrage there could still be a feeling of "my poor child." But when the reality of your shattered dream sinks in, the feeling is more "poor me."

Find Good Friends

What do you need during the impact phase of a crisis? You need an environment that will help your grieving and hurting heart to heal. Stay away from people who are full of advice and who say, "I told you so" or "Spiritual Christians get over their hurt sooner than others." The people who can help you most are those who are most empathetic.

They don't shock easily, but accept your human feelings.

They are not embarrassed by your tears.

They do not give unwanted advice.

They are warm and affectionate with you according to your needs.

They help you recall your strengths when you have forgotten you have strengths.

They trust you to be able to come through this difficult time.

They treat you like an adult who can make your own decisions.

They may become angry with you but do not attack your character.

They respect your courage and sense of determination.

They understand that grief is normal and they understand the stages of grief.

They, too, may have been through times of difficulty and can share those times with you.

They try to understand what your feelings mean to you.

They are faithful to commitments and promises.

They pray with you and for you.

They do not spiritualize and do not try to force-feed you theology and Scripture.[3]

Who do you know who would fit this list? Your spouse? A friend? A relative? It is best to find people with these qualities and cultivate their friendship before a crisis hits. But remember that we draw those kinds of people to us as we demonstrate those qualities ourselves.

Let's summarize now what happens to you during the impact phase.

- This phase will normally take a few hours to a few days. But because of the suddenness or seriousness of a crisis, or because of multiple crises occurring at one time, it could either extend longer or else be returned to—so don't let anyone else put a time limit on you.
- You want to either face and fight the situation or flee from it.
- Your thinking will be somewhat numb and disoriented.
- You will search for whatever it is that you have lost, often by reminiscing.
- You will need people to accept your feelings.

As one writer has put it,

Recovery from loss is like having to get off the main highway every so many miles because the direct route is under reconstruction. The road signs reroute you through little towns you hadn't expected to visit and over bumpy roads you hadn't wanted to bounce around on. You are basically traveling in the appropriate direction. On the map, however, the course you are following has the look of shark's teeth instead of a straight line. Although you are gradually getting there, you sometimes doubt that you will ever meet up with the finished highway.[4]

The Withdrawal-Confusion Phase

The next jag in the road is called the *withdrawal-confusion phase*. This will last for days, weeks, or even months because of the ongoing nature of a prodigal crisis. You'll feel emotionally drained. And remember, these phases overlap one another as well.

During this phase your tendency to deny your feelings is probably going to be stronger than at any other time. One reason is that your feelings now become the ugliest. You'll find that one emotion triggers another. You may feel intense anger at whatever has occurred, which, in some cases, brings on guilt for having such feelings. Then you'll feel shame, and the pain from these varied responses makes the desire to repress them very strong. If some of your feelings shock others, you may want to repress them even more.

Expect your feelings to run wild. This is normal. In fact, you will likely run the gamut of the following responses.

Bewilderment: "I never felt this way before."

Danger: "I feel so scared. Something terrible is going to happen to my child."

Anger: "I'm angry at the whole world. My child, my spouse, the school, the church, myself, and God!"

Confusion: "I can't think clearly. My mind doesn't seem to work."

Impasse: "I'm stuck. Nothing I do seems to help. She won't respond to me."

Desperation: "I've got to do something, but I don't know what to do."

Apathy: "Nothing can help me. What's the use of trying."

Helplessness: "I can't cope by myself. Please help me."

Urgency: "I need help *now*."

Discomfort: "I feel so miserable and unhappy."

During this phase your thinking will reflect a certain amount of uncertainty and ambiguity. You just aren't sure what to think or do.

You will alternate between bargaining and detachment. Bargaining involves wishful thinking: "If only this hadn't happened"; "if only I could recapture what we used to have as a family"; "perhaps I can take the consequences for what my son did."

This type of thinking could move to the detachment level. You feel a need to detach yourself from the problem. You distance yourself by saying, "He should have known better. It's his life now." "She made her bed. She's got to deal with the results." "No son of mine would do that. He's not my son anymore." "No more help from me if that's the way she lives her life." You do this to ease the pain of your loss.

Around home you may find yourself vacillating between doing tasks that need to be done and then reflecting and reminiscing upon how things used to be. You'll recall some of the enjoyable times with your child. You may feel anger at having to give up what you used to have. You're trying to protect yourself from the emptiness that this crisis brings. And in your attempt to bring back what is gone, you may tend to distort and glorify the past family life together. You may see it as being better than it was. We do this to help us face the future.

During this time, you need the assistance of caring friends and relatives to help you organize your life. You will find that you may need assistance in planning your day, arranging appointments, keeping the house or job in order, and so on. Don't be hard on yourself for this apparent defect in your life. This is a normal transition that you need to pass through.

Just expect to hear statements you'd rather not hear. It's difficult to respond to these people the way we would like to because of our traumatized state, but perhaps they would learn not to say such painful things if someone spoke up and said, "That's not true and it's not helpful. If you want to be helpful I would appreciate it if you would . . . ." We often excuse these people as well-meaning, but their intent is sometimes questionable. Sometimes they're just reflecting their own anxiety, fear, or lack of having dealt with issues in their own lives. Remember, this is generally *not advice coming from experts.*

Consider some typical clichés we hear from others when we go through a prodigal crisis.

"Be Strong" Clichés
You must be strong for the other children.
Support groups are for wimps.
You've just got to get hold of yourself!
Others have held up well. You can too.
Cheer up.
No sense crying over spilled milk.
This is normal behavior for boys.

"Hurry Up" Clichés
You're not your old self.

Out of sight, out of mind.
Time will heal.
I just don't understand your behavior.
Life goes on.
No sense dwelling on the past.

"Guilt" Clichés

If you look around, you can always find someone who is worse off
than you.
This is the work of the devil (meaning that if you had a closer
relationship with God, the devil couldn't have had his
way).
If I were you, I'd do it this way.
Count your blessings.
If you had been a better Christian, this wouldn't have happened.
Think of all your precious memories.

"God" Clichés

God did this to show how powerful He can be in your life.
It was God's will.
God never gives us more than we can handle.
God helps those who help themselves.

"Discounting" Clichés

I know just how you feel.
Silence is golden.
If there's anything I can do, just call me.

Those who talk to you in this manner need to be avoided or educated!
During this phase, when the numbness has worn off, you begin to feel the
pain of hearing comments such as these.

To summarize, in the withdrawal-confusion phase, remember that:

• This phase will last for days, weeks, or even longer.
• Your response will be emotional. You may feel anger, fear, guilt, rage.
  (Take another look at the *Ball of Crisis and Grief* feelings on p. 28.)
• Your thought life will be ambiguous and uncertain.
• You'll vacillate from bargaining to working on detaching yourself
  from your child's situation or even your child.

• During this time of puzzled searching for a way out of the difficulty, you need some specific guidance and support from others.

The Adjustment Phase

The third phase is called the *adjustment phase*. This will take weeks or months to work through and the emotional responses you will experience during this time are more hopeful. Some depression may come and go, but your positive attitudes have started to form. You may begin to talk about the future. With help, you're better able to focus on the other children, your spouse, your job, and perhaps you may even have some hope for your child. You have now just about completed your detachment from what you lost. You are looking around for something new to bring into your life to which you can develop an attachment. However, be careful not to base this upon changes your child may seem to be making, as this puts you at his mercy. Safer attachments may include a deeper relationship with the Lord, a support group, or helping others. Too often our prodigal takes all of our energy. It's time to reinvest.

"What happens now" has started to take on some special significance for you. You have been in and through the depths of the valley. You are now climbing up the side of the mountain. Continue to be prepared for the opinions and advice of others and sift through what you hear. Others may not see the value of what you are doing now. They may feel that you are making a drastic mistake in this new step. Some will advise you to cut yourself off from your child, while others will suggest bending over backwards to accept her.

Don't make any of your decisions during your down times. Wait until there is hope. And don't despair because your feelings fluctuate. Your insight will return and your objectivity can help you process information and new suggestions. The Bible and its teaching can assist you in your decisions during this phase. You're more receptive and capable of dealing with spiritual insights now. Prior to this, Scripture and prayer resources were there to support and sustain you. Now is the time to seek definite answers and direction through the teaching and reading of the Word, as well as through prayer.

To summarize this phase, *remember*:

• This phase may last weeks or even months.
• Your positive thinking has started.

- You are involved in problem solving.
- You are searching for something new in your life.
- The kind of support you most need at this time is spiritual guidance.

The Reconstruction-Reconciliation Phase

The fourth period (which can take the longest) is the *reconstruction-reconciliation phase*. A key element here is the spontaneous expression of hope. Your sense of confidence has returned and you can make plans again. You are able to make the conscious decision not to engage in self-pity anymore. Self-initiative for progress and new attachments are occurring. In existence now are new activities, new people from a support group, new ways of responding to your child and his situation, and new spiritual and personal insights. If any of your anger and blame created difficulty during this crisis, now is the time for reconciliation. (See chapter 12 for more information on reconciliation).

A sign of the resolution of a crisis is the newness of life you feel. A crisis is an opportunity for you to gain new strengths, new perspectives on life, new appreciation, new values, and a new way to approach your life. You'll look at life differently and no longer take it for granted. I know. I have been through several crises in addition to the one with our daughter and have experienced all four phases. Sometimes it is possible to work through the four phases in less time than indicated. And sometimes one or two of the phases may take more time because of the prolonged issues in your prodigal's life.

The Normal Crisis Pattern

	Phase I Impact	Phase II Withdrawal Confusion	Phase III Adjustment	Phase IV Reconstruction/ Reconciliation
		Emotional Level		
Time	Few hours to a few days	Days to weeks	Weeks to months	Months
Response	Should I stay and face it or withdraw?	Intense emotions. You feel drained. Anger, sadness, fear, anxiety, depression, rage, guilt.	Your positive thoughts begin returning along with all the emotions.	Hope has returned. Self-confidence.
Thoughts	Numb, disoriented. Insight ability limited. Feelings overwhelm.	Thinking ability limited. Uncertainty and ambiguity.	You're now able to problem solve.	Thinking is clearer.
Direction you take to regain control:	You search for what you lost.	Bargaining-wishful thinking. Detachment.	You begin looking for something new to invest in.	Progress is evident and new attachments are made to something significant.
Searching Behavior	Often reminiscing.	Puzzled, unclear.	You can now stay focused and begin to learn from your experience.	You many want to stop and evaluate where you've been and where you're going.

A crisis chart has been included at the bottom of page 35 so you can identify where you are, where you've been, and where you're going. Remember, all of us who experience a crisis travel this path.

Grief, Your Companion Through All the Phases

It is inevitable that during this crisis you will experience grief. You need to grieve; what you have experienced is a major loss. Mourning your loss is necessary to recovery. Your grief will be probably be most intense during phases two and three of your crisis, though a bit of it could be with you the rest of your life because of your shattered dreams. Be aware that we all grieve differently. Listen to the stories of how several parents experienced their grief in the withdrawal/confusion phase:

> Actually packing up my daughter's bedroom was part of my grieving. I think we grieved just as if our child had died. At times, my husband and I just sat and cried together. Everyone grieves differently. My husband could not go speak to our daughter at the cross-country meet we attended. It was just too painful for him. I wished we would have, but I had to respect his grief.

> The grief process was difficult as my husband and I handled it differently. He tended to throw himself into his work and the church. I, however, tended to withdraw from everything and everyone. I no longer wanted to be in front of the people, sharing from my heart as I had in the past. I didn't want to teach or preach anymore. I didn't want to counsel other people, feeling instead that they should "grow up and tend to their own problems since I had to"; I wanted to be left alone. I was wounded and I wanted to go off by myself to lick my wounds and not make a public display of them.
>
> My husband and I gave each other the space we needed and didn't overreact to the stress by pressuring each other with expectations. He released me from some of my responsibilities at the church, and I allowed him the hours he needed. We did not, however, neglect each other and were actually drawn together and comforted by our opposite reactions to this crisis.

> I spent a lot of time weeping for the first couple of years. And it got so I could not cry anymore. I wondered if I was callous or

what? I don't know, but that's the way it was. I literally gave it over to God and recognized we certainly weren't in control. I tried to be sensitive to my wife's feelings and assure her she was a great mother and that our daughter was making her own decisions. We grew closer and relied on each other more and more. Holding each other at night was helpful. I thank God I didn't have to do this alone—I can't imagine a single parent having to go through what we went through. Interestingly, I was memorizing James with a friend and James 1:2, "Consider it all joy, my brethren, when you encounter various trials," was a verse that I felt was a test for me. And I earnestly tried to thank God for this trial—and I believed it helped.

My wife called other women, got books and read them, and talked to any woman she thought would help her, probably because I wasn't that much of a help to her. I grieved in my heart, not because I felt I had lost a son, even though I felt those feelings, [but] what bothers me the most is that I see so much potential in my son in helping others find the Lord, and he is wasting years of his life that someday, if he lets the Lord have His way with his life, he will regret.

We banded together as a family, prayed together, fasted together. Attended all church services, never quit serving God, tithing, Bible reading, etc. We also gave each other space to work through our own feelings [and] talked about it openly. . . . We remained united in our response. We attended cell groups and joined the prodigal cell group.

My husband's (my daughter's stepfather's) grief was much different than mine. He grieved for what had happened in our family, but not to the same degree as I did. He also grieved for me. (Perhaps mostly for me.) He saw how much both my daughter and my ex-husband were hurting me and it made him sad and angry too. His emotions were in response to his love for me. He wanted to be able to make things right and didn't want to see me have to live through so much pain.

He was very sensitive and patient, letting me share my feelings and tears. He planned getaways and pitched in extra to help around the house to ease my burden. I'm not sure I was as sensitive to him as I felt he was to me. I was very unbalanced for quite some time and he really came alongside me and met my needs.

I went through various stages of grief. It hit at different times. Another "stage" was following high school graduation. (She had been living with her dad for one year with very little contact during that time.) I had always dreamed of a big celebration for my daughter's graduation. So as graduation came, with her permission and approval I planned the event. It was strained but enjoyable. Yet following the event I fell into deep, deep depression, realizing anew all the things I still needed to grieve. I needed to accept that some things I had always "expected" would NEVER happen, e.g., I would never again have the chance to experience my only daughter's senior year of high school and all the fun it could bring: homecoming (she was the queen and I didn't get to escort her; her father and stepmother walked her to the platform), making college plans and filling out applications, helping her get a car (her father bought her what she wanted, a 1960 VW bus), senior pictures, parties, academic honor banquets, packing up her room and "moving to college," the list goes on. After I faced those losses I had a new sense of release. I realized that I had always "expected" her to leave following high school graduation. I had begun years earlier preparing in my mind and heart for her to go away to college. It was the right time now to really let her go, to feel like my job was complete. It was difficult to let go prior to graduation because I felt my "parenting" job (and privileges) weren't quite over yet.

I felt devastated, sad, hurt, horror, and rejection. I got down on myself and rehashed everything I did and didn't do. Looking back, I see that our approach was too rigid, legalistic, and performance-based.

I grieved until I was through grieving. I had what I'd call a vision. I saw my heart cut open by a hatchet that our daughter wielded. My heart was bleeding and was full of pain, which seemed like an infection (poison). I asked God to clean out the infection and to heal my heart. It was a gradual process. He took the poison out and sutured my heart together again and I was healed. After over twenty-five years, she still hurts me, but I am more quickly able to run to the Lord and work through the pain.

My husband and I dealt differently with our pain. He listened a lot. We talked about our feelings and emotions and have prayed together for her.

Why am I telling you about these phases of a crisis?

1. Because by knowing what the four phases of a crisis are, you'll realize that you are *not* going crazy. You are going through a normal response to your prodigal's behavior.

2. Because by becoming aware of these phases now, some of the pain and pressure may be relieved later on. You can recall, "Oh, yes, this phase will pass and I will go into the next one."

3. Because by knowing the pattern that responses usually take, you will realize there is light at the end of the tunnel. There *is* hope.

4. Because if you understand what you are experiencing and what to expect, perhaps you can gain control of your life and the outcome a bit sooner than you would otherwise.

The Impact of a Crisis

Why do some parents seem to handle the prodigal crisis well, while others don't? Let's consider some characteristics of those who appear to have the most difficulty.

Some individuals are *emotionally fragile* to begin with, and specific events are more difficult for them to handle.

Those who have a *physical ailment or illness* will struggle because they have fewer resources upon which to draw.

The parents who tend to *deny reality* have a harder time coping with their situation. Refusing to acknowledge the truth only worsens the situation.

Some *have a tendency to eat, drink, smoke, or talk excessively.* When a crisis enters these people's lives, they seem to regress into self-medication through their mouths. This refusal to face the real problem can continue after the crisis is over and can actually help to create an additional crisis for the person.

Other parents have an *unrealistic approach to time.* They may crowd the time dimensions of a problem or extend the time factors way into the future. They may want the problem to be "fixed" right away, feel frantic to have it resolved before it reasonably can be; or they may delay addressing it. Delay temporarily avoids the discomfort of reality but ultimately enlarges the problem. People who struggle with *excessive guilt* over their prodigal will have difficulty coping with a crisis. They tend to blame themselves for the situation, which increases feelings of guilt, thus further immobilizing them.

People who *place blame* have a difficult time coping with a crisis. They do not focus on what the problem is; rather, they focus on who caused the problem. Their approach is to find enemies, either real or imagined, and project blame onto them. It may be the child's friends, school, other parent, or even the church.

Those who tend to be *overly dependent or overly independent* also do not cope well with a crisis. Such parents either turn away from offers of help or become clinging vines. One other characteristic has a bearing on all the others—*how the person perceives God.*

The way we perceive God is a reflection of our theology and will affect how we cope with parental crises. Our lives are based upon our theology, yet so many people are frightened by it.

When we go through difficult times, we are often forced to reevaluate what we truly believe. Unfortunately, many determine what they believe by what they are going through. They allow their theology to be determined by their circumstances. When they hit the problems of life, they seem to negate the promises of God and begin to wonder if He cares!

Sometimes crises can change our view of God. Max Lucado describes the process well:

> There is a window in your heart through which you can see God. Once upon a time that window was clear. Your view of God was crisp. You could see God as vividly as you could see a gentle valley or hillside. The glass was clean, the pane unbroken.
>
> You knew God. You knew how he worked. You knew what he wanted you to do. No surprises. Nothing unexpected. You knew that God had a will, and you continually discovered what it was.
>
> Then, suddenly, the window cracked. A pebble broke the window. A pebble of pain.
>
> Perhaps the stone struck when you were a child and a parent left home—forever. Maybe the rock hit in adolescence when your heart was broken. Maybe you made it into adulthood before the window was cracked. But then the pebble came.
>
> Was it a phone call? "We have your daughter at the station, you'd better come down here."

Was it a letter on the kitchen table? "I've left. Don't try to reach me. Don't try to call me. It's over. I can't stand living here. I've run away."

Was it a diagnosis from the doctor? "I'm afraid the news about your son is not very good. He has AIDS. It was his lifestyle."[5]

A Biblical View of Suffering

We all wish we could avoid suffering and just sail through life without pain. We see suffering as being the exception in life. But perhaps it is the norm, and the suffering-free times are exceptions. Consider the following themes found in the Scripture.[6]

1. The Certainty of Suffering

Faithful Christians are sure to suffer. In this world you will suffer.

Peter said, "Dear friends, do not be surprised at the painful trial you are suffering, as though something strange were happening to you." (1 Peter 4:12)

Jesus said, "In this world you will have trouble." (John 16:33)

2. The Calling to Suffer

We find in the Bible a call to suffer that chafes against the call to comfort we find glorified in much of today's Christian culture.

For it has been granted to you on behalf of Christ not only to believe on him, but also to suffer for him. (Phil. 1:29)

To this you were called, because Christ suffered for you, leaving you an example, that you should follow in his steps. (1 Peter 2:21)

In fact, everyone who wants to live a godly life in Christ Jesus will be persecuted. (2 Tim. 3:12)

Consider it pure joy, my brothers, whenever you face trials of many kinds. (James 1:2)

If you are insulted because of the name of Christ, you are blessed, for the Spirit of glory and of God rests on you. (1 Peter 4:14)

3. The Purpose of Suffering

People can handle almost any amount of evil and suffering if they believe it is for a purpose. The Bible helps us understand that there is no such thing as meaningless suffering as describes its many purposes:

- So that we will rely not upon ourselves but upon God. (2 Cor. 1:9)

- So that we may become more sensitive to others, that we can comfort them with the comfort we ourselves have received. (2 Cor. 1:4; Luke 22:31-33).

- So that through our sufferings, the saving grace of God will reach more and more people. (2 Cor. 4:15)

- So that God may receive praise. (1 Peter 1:6-7)

- So that our character may be developed. (Rom. 5:3-5)

4. The Comfort in Suffering

Can we become all that God wants us to be without affliction? The Bible indicates that the answer is no. We need the grace of affliction. Yes, trials and tribulations are painful at the time, and we should never seek them out. Yet, when they come, they come as the sweet fragrance of God's grace to help us grow, mature, and stay on the right path. King David understood that affliction is actually a blessing:

> It was good for me to be afflicted
> So that I might learn your decrees . . .
> Before I was afflicted I went astray,
> But now I obey your word . . .
> I know, O Lord, that your laws are righteous,
> And in faithfulness you have afflicted me . . .
> If your law had not been my delight,
> I would have perished in my affliction.
> (Ps. 119:71, 67, 75, 92)

It's true that once a crisis hits, your life will never be exactly the way it was, especially in the case of some prodigal problems.

A crisis is like a bomb that sprays its lethal projectiles all around without regard for anyone standing in the way. The haunting words of an old children's game reflect the fallout of a crisis:

Ring around the rosie,
Pocketful of posies
Ashes, ashes,
All fall down.

But if we let Him, God uses the fallout from crises to refine and hone our sense of His love toward us and His sovereignty in our lives.

A crisis will either destroy us or transform us. Surviving parents are the parents who understand the typical ways of responding to a crisis and the stages they will experience as they walk through it.[7]

....

1. Lloyd H. Ahlems, *Living with Stress* (Ventura, Calif.: Regal Books, 1978), adapted from various portions.
2. Aleksandr Solzhenitsyn, as quoted in Barry Johnson, *Choosing Hope* (Nashville: Abingdon, 1988), p. 178.
3. Ann Kaiser, *Living Through a Personal Crisis* (New York: Ballantine Books, 1984), p. 66, 67, adapted.
4. Kaiser, pp. 71-72, adapted.
5. Max Lucado, *In the Eye of the Storm* (Nashville: Word, Inc., 1991), pp. 105-6.
6. Patrick Morley, *Seven Seasons of a Man's Life* (Grand Rapids, Mich.: Zondervan Publishing House, 1997), pp. 246-251, adapted.
7. This chapter has been adapted from *Resilience* by H. Norman Wright (Ann Arbor, Mich.: Servant Publications, 1997).

CHAPTER THREE

You Feel Such Guilt!

E ver feel as if you're the only parent with a child not toeing the
mark? You're not alone; in fact, you're in pretty good company.

> They felt good eyes upon them
> and shrank within—undone;
> good parents had good children
> and they—the wandering one.
>
> The good folk never meant
> to act smug or condemn,
> but having prodigals
> just "wasn't done" with them.
>
> Remind them gently, Lord
> how You have trouble with Your children, too.[1]

Guilt—it's a constant companion to the parent of a prodigal. You'll
kick it out and it will return, probably again and again. Much of it comes
from second-guessing yourself. You look back over the years and try to

analyze what you did, didn't do, didn't do enough of, or did too much of. You try to reconstruct situations, encounters, conversations, events, teaching you heard and applied, teaching you heard and didn't apply, searching for some answer, some reason, some solution to what happened! But the answers are hard to find. For one thing, our memories are often selective. What we do remember is just our own one-sided perspective, and even that isn't always accurate. The longer the time span between now and what you're trying to recall, the greater the haziness of the details. And as a hurting parent, your tendency is to overlook the good times or the things you did right. Instead, you're looking for the deficiencies, and the more you do so, the further you plunge into the depths of guilt.

Where Did I Go Wrong?

It's the child whose behavior is lacking, but too often it's the parents who carry the load of guilt and self-blame. Perhaps the more determined you are that your child will be a certain way, the more intense the pain. I've heard parents say, "What went wrong?" And in time I hear, "What did I do wrong? Where did I blow it?" Mothers, especially, feel this way and are quicker to admit it than fathers. The author of *Mother, I Have Something to Tell You* talked about this universal struggle:

> The mother's dilemma in a nugget: "I did something or I didn't do something." What mother can ever be sure that what she is doing—or not doing—with her child is right, unmistakably, irrefutably right, at any given moment?
>
> This guilt has been unfairly augmented by so-called experts. Dr. Paula Caplan and Dr. Ian Hall-McCorquodale, of the Ontario Institute for Studies in Education, recently reviewed one hundred and twenty-five articles in journals of clinical psychology from 1970, 1976, and 1982. They found "mother-blaming" rampant, regardless of the sex of the author, the type of journal, and the year of publication. Seventy-two kinds of disorders were directly attributed to mothers. Mothers were related to a child's problems five times as often as fathers.
>
> The time has come to take mothers off the hook. Successful mothering depends on a mysterious anagram of personality and circumstance. What works with one child will not work with his sister. In the families described here, children who are now happy, independent, and productive grew up with brothers or sisters

whose lives seemed to their mothers to be, to use a word that keeps recurring in these interviews, "wasted." And, as different as the children have turned out, the mother is not aware of having treated them in the least differently when they were growing up. In fact, the child who comes to grieve the mother most may have been the one who showed the most promise. Because they are curious and courageous, the most promising children often behave the least traditionally. They have everything going for them— intelligence, talent, concern for others, an appetite for life. They are accustomed to success. Small wonder that these young people are so often the ones who find defying tradition easy and tempting.

When they succeed, their mother does not take the credit. When they fail, should she take the blame? Whatever other questions a mother may ask the experts as she begins to pay attention to her child as he really is, the one great spoken or unspoken question for every mother is, "Is it my fault?"

The answer she gets depends on which expert she asks.[2]

It's normal to look at yourself and begin to blame. Yet even though we are all imperfect as parents (and some perhaps more than others!), *the rebellion of your children doesn't mean you're a failure as a parent.* Your head may agree with that, but your feelings don't.

You may be like most parents who, throughout their parenting, have struggled with a sense of desperation that periodically rises within you. It's seen in the questions you keep asking yourself: "What if I fail? What if I'm not a perfect parent?" Well, relax! I have a perfect answer for your dilemma. There is no such creature as a perfect parent. And there are some facts that need to be faced:

You have failed in the past. So have I.
You are failing now in some way. So am I.
You will fail in the future. So will I.
You were not perfect in the past. Neither was I.
You are not perfect now. Neither am I.
You will not be perfect in the future. Neither will I.

I like what pastor David Seamands says about those of us who struggle with the question of failure:

To ask the question, "What if I fail?" is once again to attach strings to God's unconditional love and to change the nature of grace as undeserved and unearned favor. If your failure could stop grace, there would never be any such thing as grace. For the ground of grace is the cross of Christ, and on the cross we were all judged as total failures. It was not a question of an occasional failure here and there. As far as our ability to bridge the moral canyon and win the approval of a Holy God, we are all total failures. In the cross we were all examined and we all flunked completely.[3]

In spite of failing, we are still loved and accepted by God. We are still recipients of His undeserved grace. That's good news for all of us.[4]

All parents fail at one time or another. I have made mistakes. So have you. But *why do we equate mistakes with failure?* They are not one and the same. You and I will make plenty of mistakes. As parents we are all amateurs and learn as we go along. Failure occurs when we *don't* learn and make a course correction as a result of our mistakes. We also fail when we give up the fight and surrender to the status quo.

What about you? Have you asked this question? Often it becomes imprinted in the mind of the parent as he or she reruns it again and again. "*Did* I do something wrong? *What* did I do wrong? *Where* did I fail them?" We feel as though it's our fault even though we can't put our finger on the reason. We feel as though it's our fault and no comment from others will change our mind.

We know that we aren't the only influence in our child's life . . . but that doesn't matter. We understand children have a sinful nature and a built-in bent toward rebellion. We understand that genetic makeup has some influence, as does the tempting world around them. We know this and may have even tried to console other parents with these thoughts. But when something happens with our own child, all this theory seems to lose its strength. It's hard for us to grasp the fact that we didn't have the influence we thought we did. Have you ever thought or said something similar to these statements?

"I did something wrong, which is why he's gay."

"I did something wrong, which is why he's using drugs."

"I did something wrong, which is why she's living with that reject!"

"I did something wrong, which is why he's schizophrenic."

"I did something wrong, which is why she attempted suicide."

A NOTE FROM

Linda Brown

*And whoso shall receive one such little child
in my name receiveth me.   Matthew 18:5*

V.B.S. 1990

*And whoso shall receive one such little child
in my name receiveth me.   Matthew 18:5*

V.B.S. 1990

A NOTE FROM

Linda Brown

*And whoso shall receive one such little child
in my name receiveth me.   Matthew 18:5*

V.B.S. 1990

And whoso shall receive one such little child in my name receiveth me.   Matthew 18:5

V.B.S. 1990

*And whoso shall receive one such little child
in my name receiveth me.   Matthew 18:5*

V.B.S. 1990

"I did something wrong, which is why he dropped out of school."

"I did something wrong, which is why she got AIDS."

"I did something wrong, which is why he joined a cult."

"I did something wrong, which is why she ran away from home."

There will be some children who hold us responsible for what has happened to them. There will be some who say we had nothing to do with it. There will be some who say, "Who cares?" Former presidential candidate and U.S. Senator George McGovern wrote about his daughter, Terry. She struggled with alcoholism for years, and at forty-five, while in an alcoholic stupor, fell into a snowbank and froze to death. It didn't matter that he knew there was a genetic basis for this condition or that the disease ran in his family or that she had a mind of her own; he still asked himself the convicting questions, "What could I have done differently? How could I have been more involved or concerned?"

Intellectually, you may believe and agree that your child's problem is not your fault. But that belief won't prevent the contractions of regret and self-blame from occurring. Logic doesn't always prevail.

Who can explain why four children in a family have healthy attitudes and are morally responsible—but one rebels? We're dealing with birth order, personality differences, neurological structure, things like an inordinate amount of peer pressure, and a child's own free will. We have to bear in mind, also, that if we are raising our kids to be Christians and reflect that value system, we are raising them to be minority individuals in a hostile environment.

Every parent of a prodigal experiences guilt. But one of the hardest situations to handle is when the consequences of the prodigal's behavior affect not only the child, but society. If a child's behavior results in a prison term, the parents are uniquely pained in several ways.

There is the personal shame and disappointment over the child's moral failure.

There is the pain stemming from the parents' empathy for their child's pain.

There is pain over the hurt their child has inflicted on others—the victims, other family members, and friends who trusted or invested in this child.

There is the pain of the disruption of the parents' lives while their child is incarcerated. Their focus is on visitation of the child, safety, calls, correspondence, etc.

Regardless of the way in which their child's rebellion is expressed, I've heard parents say they didn't give their child enough opportunities, talk to their child about feelings enough, invite their child's friends over enough, home-school enough, send him or her to Christian school or church enough . . . the list goes on and on. Do you find yourself sprinkling your thoughts with phrases like "should have," "shouldn't have," "wish I had," "wish I hadn't," "too much", "not enough"? If so, guilt is sucking you down like quicksand. Answer the following questions as truthfully as you can.

	Yes	No
Do you think you were committed enough to your child?		
Do you think you were attentive enough to your child?		
Do you think you were helpful enough with classwork?		
Do you think you were loving enough with your child?		
Do you think you spent enough time with your child?		
Do you think you gave your child sufficient praise?		
Do you think there was sufficient discipline?		
Do you think you were firm enough with your child?		
Do you think you allowed enough freedom for your child?		
Do you think you sufficiently encouraged for your child?		

Look at each question you answered no and ask yourself what *would* have been enough. And if you had done things differently, would it really have kept your child from going the direction he or she went? What standard are you using to measure whether or not it was enough? How can you possibly measure that?

In some cases there is probably never enough. Is it possible for you to go back and say, "Wait a minute. I *did* give enough in that area"? Sometimes a child's desire (rather than need) is insatiable. No matter what or how much you give, it's never enough.

We victimize ourselves through our own self-criticism. The belief that "there must have been something different I could have done" will cripple our future. And sometimes the problem of self-criticism spreads wider than just within our own families. Are there people in your life besides your child for whom you feel that you have done either too little or too much? If so, have they said anything about it? If nothing has been said, don't assume the worst! And if something has been said, ask yourself whether that person is an expert on the subject.

Many of us have a driving need for others to confirm that what we have done was right. But when we do so, we put ourselves at their mercy. We're giving them control over us.[5]

Beliefs That Need Challenging

At the heart of this problem is a set of beliefs and expectations that need to be challenged. Let's look at a couple of them and see whether or not they apply to you, and whether they might be contributing to a pervasive sense of guilt or shame in your life.

- Do you feel that what others think about you is so important that they *must* think about you in a positive way?
- If someone disapproves of the way you raised your child or of what your child does, does that mean you're a failure?

Sometimes we get caught up in wanting others not to know what has happened. We don't want them to see us in such an unflattering light.

If you feel upset over what your child has done or is doing, is it concern for your child, for yourself, or for what others will think or believe about you? We can't please everyone else, nor are we called to do so. If we try to, we've set for ourselves an impossible task. I like the statement that Candace and William Backus suggest that we say to ourselves:

Although I do care reasonably about the reactions and opinions of people I value, I can stand it if they don't agree with me. So when I believe I'm in God's will, the verdicts of most other people matter very little or not at all.[6]

Here are some other truths to remind yourself of when you're battling shame:

My child's problems do *not* mean I'm a failure, and I will stop telling myself it's the end of the world when someone else knows about our troubles or disapproves of me because of them.

I don't have to have a guarantee that every person I know thinks that I and my family are perfect.

People don't have to think I'm a better parent than I actually am.

It's more important for me to be open and truthful than to fabricate a false public image.[7]

In her novel *Ordinary Love,* Jane Smiley talks about trying to accept the mystery of her children, of the various ways they diverge from parental expectations. She says that over the past twenty years of her life, she has learned to embrace the possible and not mourn the past.

This is a healthy perspective. It's far better than the grandiose notion some parents have that they will shape their children's nature like a lump of clay and control their destiny. Many parents strive to make their children into refined replicas of themselves, but without the pain they themselves had to endure as they developed. The fantasy-filled blueprints that parents work from in their children's development need to be discarded.[8]

Ezekiel 18 is helpful in assessing blame for the rebellious behavior of grown children. God's way of looking at that situation is clear:

"The word of the Lord came to me: 'What do you people mean by quoting this proverb about the land of Israel: "The fathers eat sour grapes, and the children's teeth are set on edge"? As surely as I live, declares the Sovereign Lord, you will no longer quote this proverb in Israel. For every living soul belongs to me, the father as well as the son—both alike belong to me. The soul who sins is the one who will die.'" (Ezek. 18:1-4) Then in verse 20, Ezekiel concludes, "The son will not share the guilt of the father, nor will the father share the guilt of the son. The righteousness of the righteous man will be credited to him, and the wickedness of the wicked will be charged against him."

If you have begun to doubt your parenting skills, or if you are wondering whether your child's rebellion is all your fault, get hold of a book called *Relief for Hurting Parents* by Buddy Scott and read the section in Part 1 titled "Encouragement for Fair and Reasonable Christian Parents." In fewer than ten paragraphs, he makes great strides in restoring parents' confidence in themselves and stands them back on their feet. Here's the way the section begins:

> The misbehaviors of our children do not necessarily indicate that we are failures as parents. Our worth as parents does not hinge on choices of our children.[9]

Your family isn't the only one ever to be traumatized. So was God's, and right from the beginning. He loved Adam and Eve, but He lost them. He spent time with them, but they succumbed to temptation. He confronted them, and they blamed others. They also blamed God. When confronted about his sin, Adam said, "The woman *you gave to me* did it." God understands what you're experiencing. He gave Adam and Eve a perfect environment, perfect teaching, and perfect love, and there was still no guarantee that they would choose to follow His guidelines.

If there's one passage I've heard used and misused and misinterpreted time and again, it's Proverbs 22:6: "Train a child in the way he should go, and when he is old he will not turn from it." God never intended that verse to be a guarantee that children raised faithfully would be godly. In fact, the writers of Proverbs were fully aware that godly parents might have ungodly children. Otherwise, they would not have said, "Whoever loves wisdom makes his father rejoice, but a companion of harlots wastes his wealth" (Prov. 29:3, NKJV). This proverb and others like it (for an example, see 10:5) face reality: Children can reject their parents' moral and spiritual training.

The writers also admitted that children may curse their parents: "There is a generation that curses its father, and does not bless its mother. There is a generation that is pure in its own eyes, yet is not washed from its filthiness" (Prov. 30:11-12, NKJV).

Children, according to the Book of Proverbs, may also despise their parents (see 15:20) and mock them (see 30:17). Children raised in a godly home may waste their parents' money (see 28:24) and even refuse to help a widowed mother in need of food and housing (see 19:26).

The writers of Proverbs reflected life as they experienced it (after humanity's fall into sin) and not as a fantasy existence. So what do we make of Proverbs 22:6?

The proverbs were never intended to be absolute promises from God. Instead, they're probabilities of things that are likely to occur. The primary author of Proverbs, Solomon, was the wisest man on earth at that time. His purpose was to convey his divinely inspired observations on the way human nature and God's universe work. He was saying that a given set of circumstances can generally be expected to produce certain consequences. Many people have taken numerous passages out of that context and made them to stand alone as promises from God. But how, then, can we explain why so many other proverbs do not inevitably prove accurate?

Lazy hands make a man poor, but diligent hands bring wealth. (10:4)

The fear of the Lord adds length to life, but the years of the wicked are cut short. (10:27)

No harm befalls the righteous, but the wicked have their fill of trouble. (12:21)

Plans fail for lack of counsel, but with many advisers they succeed. (15:22)

Gray hair is a crown of splendor; it is attained by a righteous life. (16:31)

The lot is cast into the lap, but its every decision is from the Lord. (16:33)

A tyrannical ruler lacks judgment, but he who hates ill-gotten gain will enjoy a long life. (28:16)

I'm sure you can think of exceptions to these and other proverbs. They appear to represent likelihoods, rather than absolutes with God's personal guarantee attached.[10]

In the original Hebrew, the phrase "in the way that he should go" reflects the thought that parents need to consider the particular child's stage of development and unique personality. *The Amplified Version* says, "In keeping with his individual gifts or bent." Rather than teaching that every child is to be responded to in the same way, this verse urges parents to train their child to love God and serve Him in accordance with the child's unique gifts and temperament.

Dr. Gleason Archer summarizes the parent's duties and their realistic expectations this way:

This type of training implies a policy of treating children as even more important than one's own personal convenience or social life away from home. It means impressing on them that they are very important persons in their own right because they are loved by God, and because He has a wonderful and perfect plan for their lives. Parents who have faithfully followed these principles and practices in rearing their children may safely entrust them as adults to the keeping and guidance of God and feel no sense of personal guilt if the child later veers off course. They have done their best before God. The rest is up to each child himself.[11]

If you follow the advice in Proverbs 22:6, there's a good probability that children will either remain true to this instruction all their lives or return to God's teachings as they mature. Remember, though, that is only a probability, *not* a certainty. What's important is that you understand the uniqueness of each child's personality and adapt your responses to that uniqueness.

Many parents might continue to feel guilty when they read Proverbs 22:6 because they hear it saying they can expect their children to be converted only if they're perfect parents. But that line of thinking ignores the biblical passages assuring them that if they try to live godly lives, God will bless them.

God does not require or expect you to be perfect. He knows that's impossible. He asks only for your best effort.

I've heard parents quote other Scripture passages in an effort to extract a promise from God that their children will either remain true to Christian principles or return to the faith. Some people think, *If only I had more faith, my child would believe. After all, Jesus said, "Ask and it will be given to you; seek and you will find" (Luke 11:9). It's my fault, because I have so little faith.*[12]

Dr. James Kennedy described what he has seen:

Some parents attempt to use "praise power" to manipulate or force God to touch their children's lives. They stand up in prayer meetings and say, with great emotion, "Father, I praise you because you have saved Susan. I praise you because she is a believer in your sight. I praise you because she is your daughter. Please manifest this truth in her life so I might praise you for that as well."

Still other parents who are more traditional fall back upon the covenant promises of infant baptism. These parents maintain, "I had John baptized and made him a child of God. God never loses one of His children. He tells us this in the parable of the Good Shepherd. He must bring John to faith and repentance or He has broken His promise."

Each of these approaches assumes that finite man can force the infinite God to act. This is a misunderstanding of the relationship between God and man. Ritualistic views of God teach that the divine Spirit must respond to certain words and actions of man just as members of the occult and priests of primitive religions utter certain words and incantations to make their gods act. "Abracadabra and your wish is granted!"[13]

But biblical faith is much more complicated than that type of thinking. Our God is the personal Lord of the universe. He is working out His plan of redemption through Jesus Christ according to His perfect will. God is sovereign in our salvation, and He grants it according to His mercy upon whom He chooses (see Rom. 9–11; Eph. 1).

Our sovereign Lord can be touched by our prayers. He allows Himself to be influenced by them. But we can never force Him to act. We need to hope that He will act, yet always be ready to accept His decision with peace and submission—and to bear in mind that the choices of our own children may interfere in His will.[14]

Confirm, O Lord, that word of Thine
That heavenly word of certainty,
Thou gavest it; I made it mine,
Believed to see.

And yet I see not; he, for whom
That good word came in Thy great love,
Is wandering still, and there is room
For fear to move.

O God of Hope, what though afar
From all desire that wanderer seems
Thy promise fails not; never are
Thy comforts dreams.

—Amy Carmichael

....

1. Larry Crabb, *Connecting* (Nashville: Word Publishing, 1997), p. XIII.
2. Jo Brans, *Mother, I Have Something to Tell You* (New York: Doubleday, 1987), p. 85.
3. Dr. David Seamands, *Freedom from the Performance Trap* (Wheaton, Ill.: Victor Books, 1988), p. 117.
4. Seamands, p. 117, adapted.
5. William and Candace Backus, *What Did I Do Wrong?* (Minneapolis: Bethany House Publishers, 1990), pp. 37, 38, adapted.
6. Backus, pp. 42-43.
7. Ibid.
8. Sidney Callahan, *Parents Forever* (New York: Crossroad, 1992), pp. 20-22, adapted.
9. Buddy Scott, *Relief for Hurting Parents* (Lake Jackson, Texas: Allon Publishing, 1994), p. 15.
10. James Dobson, *Parenting Isn't for Cowards* (Waco, Texas: Word, 1987), pp. 184-85, adapted.
11. Gleason L. Archer, *Encyclopedia of Bible Difficulties* (Grand Rapids, Mich.: Zondervan, 1982), p. 253.
12. James Kennedy, *Your Prodigal Child* (Nashville: Thomas Nelson, 1988), pp. 42-43, adapted.
13. Kennedy, p. 44.
14. Kennedy, p. 45, adapted.

CHAPTER FOUR

How Do You
Handle the Responses
of Others?

I waited for days, even weeks before I could bring myself to tell anyone about our child," Doris said. "I used to think it wasn't because I was ashamed or embarrassed or anything, but I guess I did have those feelings. I don't know why I felt that way. Maybe I felt John's rebellion was my fault, even though I knew it wasn't. It couldn't be. I guess I was afraid of their reaction. You never know what you're going to hear. I didn't want their advice. They're not experts, and I didn't want them telling me we were bad parents."

When your child is a prodigal, there's a loss of face. If you serve in a position where others look up to you, you may feel as though you've lost your credibility. When you wonder what others may be thinking about you, you imagine the worst. You may find it difficult to be around people.

I wonder, though, how you would respond if you imagined the best? If you believed that others are for you and with you until they prove otherwise? It would certainly remove some of the pressure. Doris was experiencing the struggle of many parents: *Who can I tell about this, and what do I say?* These questions are coupled with a fear of what you might hear from others. It's a legitimate concern, because people can make comments that cut you to the core. Sometimes their remarks that sound so definite are their way of hiding their anxiety about life's uncertainties. Or they simply don't know what to say. Most people don't intend to add to your pain or guilt, but an off-hand comment can certainly do that.

This is what some parents have said about the reactions of others:

Friends as a whole were great and really helped with their concern and prayers. The only way they hurt was in not asking how we were doing more often. I think the greatest hurt I've felt over this is from family. We shared from the start what was going on and asked for their prayers, but very few have checked in with us to ask how we are doing or if there has been any change with our son. Also, only a couple of cousins have even tried to contact him or express their concern for what he is doing with his life. That hurts!

Relatives were incredibly UNHELPFUL. Our mother-in-law enabled our daughter by paying for a full semester's college tuition. She tried to tell us we needed to be more like the prodigal's father, forgiving and warmly accepting our daughter. She and several relatives told us it was the norm any more and everybody does it and it doesn't matter. One sister-in-law said it was okay for everyone to establish their own morals and ethics and wasn't that great that it was like that. Another said that if her son grew up and lived with someone without being married, it would be perfectly okay, but she would feel differently if her son became gay. That would bother her. My brothers and sisters condone my daughter's lifestyle and think we are making a lot out of nothing.

I knew people at church were praying for him and us, but felt there was no one whom I could talk with. No parent I knew of had gone through this with his or her child. They didn't have a drug-addict son. That's not to say they weren't there; they didn't let it be known. I guess I'm still angry about that. In many ways,

I believe I was surrounded by a bunch of hypocritical churchgoers.

Ironically, most of our friends could only shake their heads and say they were sorry. It was awkward for people, so for the most part, they acted like it hadn't happened. One couple actually came to us using our own words of counsel we had given them when their daughter was pregnant and out of wedlock. I was never sure if they were trying to help or just trying to turn the tables. We listened, and thanked them for their concern.

Regardless of our fears, we all have some desire to tell others our troubles in order to gain comfort and support. And some people are indeed capable of helping us carry our burdens.

I remember talking with the father of a sixteen-year-old boy who had just been arrested for possessing drugs and driving under the influence. It was discovered that the boy had been using drugs for two years. The father was crying as he said, "My wife and I felt so isolated, so alone, and we didn't know what to do. But I was afraid to let others know. You know what I was afraid of? What would others think of us. I felt like such a failure, and I was sure they'd think we had failed. I could just hear them, 'Well, they really messed up as parents. Some moral teaching they gave him!' Maybe I was afraid of hearing statements I was saying about myself. I was afraid of being judged by other parents, because I felt like such a failure, like I did something wrong or this wouldn't have happened."

What a common dilemma! Whether your child takes a detour at age twelve, sixteen, twenty-four, or thirty-four, you struggle with your feelings about yourself and expect the wrath and judgment of others. And sometimes other people *are* insensitive or judgmental. But most people are not; they're really fellow pilgrims walking the same boulder-strewn road.

You will find many people who have had similar experiences and are willing to help you work through this troubling time of life. I've taken the initiative many times in a counseling session or a seminar to describe the experiences we went through with Sheryl when she was in her early twenties. So often people are both surprised and relieved that someone else has been through what they're experiencing.

Sometimes, when parents fumble with putting their concerns and feelings into words, I say, "Could it be you're struggling with how to tell others that your child is into drugs (or alcohol, has AIDS, is living with someone, is gay, or is pregnant)? I understand your hesitation. It wasn't easy to tell others that our daughter had decided to live her life contrary to the Christian values she was raised with. It wasn't easy to say she was living with boyfriends, was using cocaine, and was becoming an alcoholic. Your dreams are shattered, and you ache inside.

"If anyone judged us, we never knew about it. I imagine some did. Some probably thought, 'How can you teach on the family when your daughter is so fouled up?' I cannot control what others think and say. As a parent, you always think about what you could have done differently. And yet often, you have done all you can to the best of your ability and have dedicated that child to the Lord. There is that element of free will that you have no control over. God knows about that. He experienced it with the first two people He ever created. He understands and wants you to experience His comfort. I wonder what your struggle is."

I have seen parents respond by breaking down and weeping, and part of the reason was the relief that someone else had been there and could understand and help. You'll find the support and comfort you need when you open your life to others.

Over the years, I've discovered that, almost without exception, people who survive a personal or family crisis give credit to another family member or friend who supported them and gave them hope. When one crisis hits, we wonder when the next one will invade our lives. Left to ourselves, our fear mounts. But friends or trusted relatives have the ability to break the cycle of despair. They can help us see that we're not helpless and will find hope somewhere. These parents share some encouraging stories of help they received:

By this time we were getting almost 100 percent of our support from the support group. None of our friends was negative about us, even when we locked our daughter out. Some of the parents of her friends were, however, very negative. Some even phoned the authorities on us. None of them phoned to ask for our side of the story!

We soon discovered our friends' honest concern did not require us to give detailed reports of our son's latest homosexual affair. Politely thanking people for their continued prayers and moving on to inquiring if there was a request we could intercede for them helped us to divert our interest to the needs of others. Rehashing the problem made us feel like we were trapped in the mire of the prodigal's pigpen experience. However, having a few confidants we could be ourselves with was a strength only God could have provided. Without judging our parenting skills or our Christianity, they helped us to carry the burden.

For the most part, I wouldn't have survived this far without the comfort and counsel of my friends. They have been a listening ear and prayer partners. I will say that those who have experienced this problem offer more help than those who have not. There is a feeling that "this will not happen to me." Funny thing, I used to think that myself.

Friends have been extremely supportive. Our closest friends are solid Christians and they have done nothing but support us. At times, we see in them the same sorrow we feel in our own hearts and you know they, too, love our son and struggle with what to do.

When you get the news about a serious problem with your child, no matter how old that child is, you're overwhelmed. You may not have the opportunity to stabilize yourself before you tell others. You'll probably share the news while you're still in turmoil. You want to tell people, and when you do, you're going to get some unedited reactions.

Three Common Reactions

You can anticipate at least three common reactions from the people you confide in.

One will be the *inability of others to accept the bad news*. There are numerous reasons for this, but the results are the same. People can't handle the situation or accept the person who has rebelled.

Often, people will verbalize sympathy and support, but their attitude and behavior communicate rejection. You end up wondering which message to believe. On the one hand, you feel them reaching out to you, but on the other, they're pulling away.

Remember that when other people are uncomfortable with your situation, they are feeling and, by their nonverbal responses, saying, "I want you 'normal' as soon as possible, or at least I want you to act that way." But you can't and won't be "normal" for some time, and no one else can determine how you should respond. This is your situation; you're upset over your tragedy and your loss. No one should rob you of your feelings and your grief. I read a statement once that describes death, but it applies to other situations as well: "When a person is born we celebrate; when they marry we jubilate; but when they die we act as if nothing has happened."[1]

Sometimes people's denial of reality comes through with statements like "Your child will grow out of it" or "Perhaps is just a one-time thing."

The more others hear about your difficulties, the greater the level of their discomfort, and they don't want your discomfort invading their lives. So they may distance themselves from you. I've seen situations in which the parents, the children, or both were no longer invited to their friends' homes, as though what they were experiencing might somehow be contagious.

When people react badly to you, it may help to explain some of the adjustments you're experiencing. Tell them you understand how uncomfortable they may feel learning about this. Don't expect them to open up and say they're having difficulty with your situation. They probably won't. But if you admit your struggle with your mixture of feelings, at least they may feel more comfortable, whether they admit anything or not.

Another reaction you'll encounter is *unsolicited advice*. When you have a child who strays, you'll get it. Everyone is an expert or knows of a similar case, and since those who care about you want to help, they give emphatic suggestions about steps you should take. Sometimes they're offended if you don't show enthusiasm and indicate you're going to follow their advice immediately. Too often, however, their suggestions are contrary to your selected plan or the advice of your counselor.

Thank them for their concern and suggestions, and let them know they are adding to the wealth of information you've been gathering. But don't commit to taking their advice. There will likely be times when nothing is working, the experts don't know what to do, or you're in a state of panic, and you may find yourself jumping from one piece of advice to another. Soon you'll be overwhelmed by a lack of follow-through on any of the suggestions. Before you take any suggestions, reflect on them. If you're still in a state of shock or crisis, let a few trusted friends help you make decisions.

Sometimes it's not just advice you have to contend with, but also the third degree. You've probably heard the questions before: "Has this happened before in your family?" "Do you have a good lawyer?"

What can you say when people criticize you? Is there a Christian way to counter the attacks of others? Listed on the next page are seven typical accusations. In the space provided, write how you would answer the person's criticism.

Accusation
I didn't know your son was on drugs. How come you never told me?
What I Would Say

Accusation
You and your wife are such nice people. I can't believe your daughter is actually an alcoholic.
What I Would Say

Accusation
I understand your child is a real terror at school. Don't you ever discipline him?
What I Would Say

Accusation
Your child is in trouble with the law and *you're* teaching Sunday School?
What I Would Say

Accusation
I understand your married son is having an affair with another woman. Don't you think you should talk to him and tell him what he's doing is wrong? After all, you *are* his parent.
What I Would Say

Accusation
Well, your son may be in jail, but at least you have your other children at home. I hope nothing goes wrong with them.
What I Would Say

Accusation
I'm sorry to hear your son wandered off from the way you raised him. This must be a shock.
What I Would Say

Sometimes the accusations are so absurd you may feel like giving an absurd answer! Other times a soft answer may cause the person to rethink his or her thoughtless comment.

Here are some suggestions of what you might say when you're faced with those all-too-common questions:

They Say . . . I didn't know your son was on drugs. How come you never told me?

You Can Say . . . It's not easy to talk about some things. Perhaps we can discuss it at another time.

They Say . . . You and your wife are such nice people. I can't believe your daughter is actually an alcoholic.

You Can Say . . . Some things are hard to accept, aren't they?

They Say . . . I understand your child is a real terror at school. Don't you ever discipline him?

But You Can Say . . . Tell me what you have heard and why you're concerned.

They Say . . . Your child is in trouble with the law and *you're* teaching Sunday School?

But You Can Say . . . I'm sorry if that offends you. Perhaps we should talk about how you feel.

They Say . . . I understand your married son is having an affair with another woman. Don't you think you should talk to him and tell him what he's doing is wrong? After all, you *are* his parent.

But You Can Say . . . What our son is doing is very upsetting to us. However, he is a grown man and must live with the consequences of his own decisions.

They Say . . . Well, your son may be in jail, but at least you have your other children at home. I hope nothing goes wrong with them.

But You Can Say . . . So do we.

They Say . . . I'm sorry to hear your son wandered off from the way you raised him. This must be a shock.

But You Can Say . . . Thank you for caring.[2]

David wrote:

> If an enemy were insulting me, I could endure it; if a foe were raising himself against me, I could hide from him. But it is you, a man like myself, my companion, my close friend, with whom I once enjoyed sweet fellowship as we walked with the throng at the house of God. (Ps. 55:12-14)

Another time, he wrote, "Even my close friend, whom I trusted, he who shared my bread, has lifted up his heel against me" (Ps. 41:9).

Yet another reaction, especially from people who really care, will be to *overwhelm you with help*. I've seen relatives and friends invade a family's boundaries and actually take away their decision-making opportunities. You need to determine how much assistance you want and establish boundaries with any intrusive friends or relatives. Most other people won't have any idea what you need or don't need until you outline it for them. They'll want to help, which is fine, but only you can determine the type and quantity of help you need.

A good starting point is to make a list of your needs and questions and then list the type of outside help you're looking for. It's all right to take time to think, to pray, and consider the options and the consequences of each. Don't let others pressure or rush you into anything.[3]

The Value of a Letter

One of the best ways I've discovered to explain your situation and your needs is to write and photocopy a letter you can give to relatives, friends, acquaintances, or anyone who asks. State what has happened, what it will be like for you, what they can expect from you, and what they can do for you. By doing this, you ease some of your pain by not having to tell the same story over and over—sometimes the repetition intensifies the pain.

Here's an example.

> Dear Friend (or whomever),
> You may have heard that we've had some difficulty with our oldest daughter. This has been very hard for my husband and me, and sometimes we're embarrassed over what has happened. Who would have expected that she would use drugs, leave high school, and live on the streets! The reason for this letter is that it's too painful to have to explain this over and over to our friends and relatives. We wish the problem would go away or that we could just hide. But it doesn't and we can't, and we don't have any idea how this is going to turn out or when it will be over.
>
> Please just keep asking us how we're doing and continue to pray for us. We probably won't be the same each time you talk with us. We could be angry one time or depressed and dejected another time. Help us to talk, and just listen. If you have some suggestions, we will consider them, and perhaps something you say will benefit us.

You may find yourself with many questions as well as feelings too. You may be shocked and find yourself angry, wishing you could talk to our daughter and knock some sense into her head. You may even wonder, as we did, where we went wrong. What could we have done differently so this would not have happened? If you hear anyone judging us, please let them know we are already doing this and need their understanding.

Please don't withdraw from us. We need your support more than ever. Pray for us as well as our daughter. We want to continue to love her, encourage her, and believe in her. Pray that we won't just concentrate on our hurt but on her needs as well. Don't be surprised if we call you from time to time and say we need to talk, or ask you to go to dinner and talk about everything other than our daughter, since we need a break.

This is a loss to us and to our other children, and it's painful. Thank you for your support.

When you take a positive, assertive step in reaching out to others and letting them know what you need, you'll gain confidence and strength. You'll feel less like a victim. Above all, talk about your feelings and concerns with family members. Don't try to protect them from the news, no matter what the problem, and be aware of the danger of neglecting them because of all the attention given to the problem.

No matter what you say, your nonverbal communication and tone of voice will convey a stronger message. If you have other children, what you tell them needs to be appropriate to their age and developmental levels. As the situation changes, you'll need to update them.

If your child is rebelling, you may be struggling with the problem of not letting that child become a role model for younger siblings. You may need the help of a counselor in knowing exactly what to say and do. One thing you can do, however, is to be careful of your own behavior around them.

Modeling provides a powerful learning experience for your child's siblings. Your children will do as you do, not say as you say. If there is a discrepancy between your words and your actions, your children will choose to imitate your actions. Actions result from attitudes, so in imitating parental actions, children incorporate parental attitudes without conscious awareness. The messages, then, that you send to your other children are the messages that you tell yourself and each other.[4]

Any of several possible events connected with your prodigal can cause you stress. Your child could be in a life-threatening situation. The HIV child could be medically stable but require intense care at home. You may be frustrated with not knowing what is wrong and may be searching for help and resources. Any of these situations can drain your limited emotional energy, time, and finances. You have only so much to give out in a twenty-four hour day. You need a certain amount of rest and nourishment. Your mind needs time to process and sort. Your bank accounts have clear limits.

When your family has a rebellious child, it's almost as if you are on an amusement park ride. When you step into the car of a roller coaster, someone else holds the controls. There are no stops or stations along the way. You are committed to being in that car until the end of the ride. The concern for your child will be a constant in your life; you're on the ride until it stops. You won't have the luxury of stopping the ride for a rest, even though you will have family business, other children, and other stresses to cope with in addition to this child.

As you consider sharing the stress of your situation with others, the person to take it to daily is the One who can provide the comfort and strength you need. You may feel overwhelmed; or you could be angry with God. In either case, don't withdraw. Don't put distance between yourself and Him. Reach out. Tell Him all your feelings. You may want to begin a daily journal in His presence to help in clarifying your feelings and progress.

Perhaps the best thing to tell others can be summed up in this phrase: "The truth; nothing but the truth."

....

1. As quoted in Bob Diets, *Life After Loss* (Tucson: Fisher Books, 1988), p. 148.
2. Marilyn McGinnis, *Parenting Without Guilt* (San Bernardino, Calif.: Here's Life Publishers, 1987), pp. 97-100.
3. Charlotte E. Thompson, *Raising a Handicapped Child* (New York: Morrow, 1986), pp. 38-41, adapted.
4. Rosemarie S. Cook, *Parenting a Child with Special Needs* (Grand Rapids, Mich.: Zondervan, 1992), p. 45, adapted.

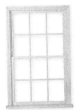

CHAPTER FIVE

How Is Your Family Responding?

W e've had our share of natural disasters over the last year or so. It seems that almost no part of the nation has escaped without a flood, earthquake, tornado, or excessive temperatures. Some of these have generated crises on a large scale, impacting communities, cities, states, or even entire sections of the country. In the worst of these crises, teams have been mobilized to assist the survivors. These teams all come in to provide support and care, but they do not all provide it in the same way. Each team assumes different roles as needed, and as they are equipped to do.

Roles Within the Family

The crisis that occurs in the family of a prodigal may not be big enough to make the news, but the family is likely to respond very much like a community when disaster strikes. Not everyone will respond in the same way. You may be surprised at the different roles the family members take.

The Protector

One of the roles that a crisis team performs is that of protecting the survivors from any more injury. In a family crisis, one member often emerges as the protector of the other members. Sometimes her goal is to insulate the others from the reality of the pain. A protector is well aware of the problem and what may need to be done, but can't be open about it. A "let's not talk about it" rule may be implemented and enforced. If other family members don't adhere to the guidelines set down by the protector, they're probably looked on as disloyal. Compliance of all other family members is expected in order to keep this family intact. The protector sees the crisis as a threat to the balance of family life, and the protector usually acts in the interest of the family. Even if the prodigal needs help and assistance at this time, her needs will be secondary to the needs of the family. A protector often feels a sense of importance, because she often receives praise from those within or outside the family. After all, the protector makes great sacrifices to preserve the family system.

Is this role truly praiseworthy, though? Not really. Insulating anyone from the reality of what is occurring isn't healthy or realistic. It retards healing and grieving, and even though a protector appears to be motivated by love, her main feeling is anger. In many ways, a protector is driven, not by love, but by the energy of anger against what the prodigal has done. Is there anyone in your family who takes this role?

The Caretaker

Another role that emerges within the family is that of caretaker. This role could be played by either a parent or a child. This person usually feels guilty over what this crisis will do to the family, as well as for what others will think about them. A caretaker works hard meeting the needs of everyone else and trying to soften the pain of the other family members. A caretaker ends up feeling special, since his desire to be helpful is appreciated by others. Unfortunately, this person ignores his own needs, since it's more fulfilling to meet the needs of others. And what is achieved never seems enough, so the caretaker works to exhaustion attempting to do even more. The more recognition he receives, the more effort is put forth. There is no balance. The caretaker may know that caring for others in this way isn't healthy, but quitting somehow feels akin to desertion of the other family members—and then who would take care of them? The caretaker may never express how he feels directly to the prodigal, but resentment is likely to build because of what has been done to the family.

Has anyone in your family assumed this role?

The Forgotten Person

Another role that can appear is that of the forgotten person. This may be a spouse/parent or a child; it could even be more than one person. Whoever it is, she ends up feeling unimportant or even left out of the family system. The forgotten person soon learns that most of the family's time and energy is devoted to the prodigal, and so to avoid the stress and protect herself, she participates less in the family, which further throws the family system out of sync. She may do this by withdrawing into solitary activities, like watching an excessive amount of TV, listening constantly to music, overeating, playing video games, spending a lot of time on the Internet, or living in a fantasy world. Unfortunately, this behavior may be reinforced by the rest of the family, who inadvertently reward this behavior since it frees them from worrying about this member of the family. The forgotten person doesn't create any trouble or additional problems. It appears to the forgotten person, as well as to others, that the family exists quite well without her. This in itself is a form of rejection, but rarely does she tell anyone how she feels. She feels miles away from the family crisis, and that's all right with her. But hurt often turns into anger, which can build into rage, which is directed toward the prodigal. Could it be that the elder son in the Parable of the Prodigal Son was a forgotten child?

In time, this person learns how to survive by living an independent life. Others acknowledge that she exists in the family, but often break promises made to her or fail to ask her opinion on family matters. If the forgotten person is a spouse, she could drift out of the family toward another individual who *is* responsive. Is there anyone who may feel like a forgotten person in your family? It happens. It may be worth discussing. Sometimes *everyone* ends up feeling like this. I've seen entire families in which each one felt as though his or her entire life was put on hold because of what had occurred. Part of the struggle came about because each one wanted to help the prodigal somehow, but also had conflicting feelings of rage toward the prodigal because of how that family member had messed up everyone else's life.[1]

In the survey we took of parents of prodigals, we asked the question, "Did the pain of the prodigal cause you to 'forget' your other children?" The responses varied:

I don't recall forgetting our other children. The only thing I remember is wanting to hold on tighter to them!

Initially, YES. While she was at home, it appeared from talking to our son later, that he felt we put all our time into dealing with the daughter and her "problems." He felt neglected by us and his sister. He still feels that she totally neglected and didn't care for him.

Yes, it did. Again, it seemed that the only way out was for our rebellious daughter to become an actual prodigal and leave.

Yes, I was so emotionally exhausted there was not much left for the other two children. All this changed when I decided it would. I stopped attending every court date and told the judge, attorney, probation officer, and social services that I would not be able to attend every court appearance. I took control of my life. Forgave myself for failing my oldest son and worked on not repeating those same errors on the other children.

No, actually it has had the opposite effect. My son provided the confirmation that I am not a worthless person. Our relationship has grown in that I feel that I should devote more time and atten-tion to his needs . . . because he is another opportunity to mold and show all those things I wanted the first one to get.

The pain caused by our prodigal only caused the rest of the family to draw closer together. We have another daughter two and a half years younger than Sue, and twin boys that were only nine at the time. They constantly asked where she was and when she was coming home. All of them love their sister, and were confused by her actions. Rather than "forget" the other children, we tended to give them a little more attention. I remember sitting down with our other daughter who was seventeen years old, and asking what she felt the problem was; asking if there were things we needed to change, and if she had the same feeling about us, the church, the Lord, as her sister had voiced. We needed her input, but asked her not to violate her sister's confidence either. This also helped her to have an outlet for her feelings, and gave us a lot of insight; no real answers, but she helped us try to understand Sue's thinking.

Parent Reactions

Taking different roles can fragment a family, but yet another hardship comes when the parents react differently to the disruption of their family life. Often, a husband and wife respond in different ways to the crisis, and they may also have different approaches on how to proceed and what to do. Their goals may be similar, but they want to take different paths to get there. This can become a major source of conflict unless there is an abundance of understanding and adapting. Here are examples of how several couples responded when asked whether they experienced disagreement:

Yes, we definitely disagreed. Two things. (1) Money—my wife kept giving our daughter money for "positive" uses. My feeling was that some or all of that money was not going to where she said it was. I cut her off completely. If it had to do with school I insisted on a check. She did not like that. This did not change until the lockout. (2) Timing of the lockout—I wanted to lock her out in January or February, when the weather would force her to think faster about her pigpen experiences. By waiting until late April I believe my wife made it too easy for our daughter.

We disagree in major ways, which has all but destroyed our family structure. I feel that our prodigal should take responsibility for her actions, including admitting the continual offenses, making restitution for wrongdoing, and at least in some way showing growth toward being a responsible person (let alone an adult). My husband feels the most important thing is to keep the lines of communication open, so he waits and does nothing about the behavior. I feel that he is enabling the bad behavior to continue and giving her the impression that it is okay to act this way. She continues to be verbally abusive, disregards any house rules, is intolerable to live with, steals from us regularly, and lies continually. I feel that I am perceived as a mean, unyielding person who doesn't care for our child.

We have not resolved anything because most of the time we are not talking.

At first we didn't agree; he was very black and white about it, wanting to send [our son] away and not allow any contact with us until he repented and turned his life around. I, on the other hand, couldn't do that and asked my spouse to reconsider what he was saying—which he did! Basically, we let the Parable of the Prodigal Son in Scripture and the way Christ deals with us when we sin direct us in to how to handle the situation.

Because I felt betrayed, I told [our son], "Go ahead and leave, I will never see you again." This comment brought extreme response from both my wife and my son. My son's response was, "I can't believe you said that, Dad." And my wife simply called my name with that tone of astonishment as only a wife can do.

My husband and I constantly disagreed over my daughter. He wouldn't let me remove her Marilyn Manson posters from the walls in her room. I wouldn't give her money. He'd give her money. I wouldn't drive her anywhere, and he'd drive her anywhere she requested. I wouldn't say we resolved these differences. They seemed to resolve themselves. I now understand he didn't/wouldn't say no to her because of his fear. He felt that she would run away and he didn't want her to.

When my daughter was twelve years old, I remarried a pastor who turned out to be very legalistic, cruel, and extremely hard and judgmental. My daughter went to church and loved the Lord before this time. My husband, after marriage, turned out to be completely different than he was before and it made my daughter leave the church and she became very rebellious, staying out all night, drinking, smoking pot, etc. It was very difficult because my husband said it was my choice to choose between him and my daughter. He was anything but an example of the Lord and his behavior was not one of a pastor. I began counseling upon my return from my honeymoon and continued throughout the marriage. My husband sent my daughter to her father's to live for a few months. The counselor told him he needed to bring her back to our home. He did, but he was always finding fault with her, and they never got along. She finally went to live with my mom until my marriage ended (approximately two years later). I read a book called *Toxic Faith* by Steve Arterburn. It helped me to see the spiritual bondage I was in at the time.

Consider what happened in Josh's family:

Josh seemed to be on his way to recovery. He'd even been leading a support group for addictive adults.

Then one night, he and some old friends from his past went out driving. He didn't really mean for it to happen, but it did. Josh started drinking again, telling himself that he would sober up tomorrow. He'd *really* quit tomorrow—this time for sure. But for now, he'd just enjoy himself . . .

Later, he saw the flashing red lights in his rearview mirror coming closer and closer. He tried to outrun the police. When they finally stopped him, he fought and kicked until the officers had no recourse but to restrain him. Josh was drunk and in trouble. Again.

After getting her son's phone call from jail, Josh's mother, Carol, anguished over him. She wondered if this would be the time he'd finally be sent to the workhouse. She hoped it would be, all the while hurting for her son. Carol could see that if Josh continued on the path he'd been on for twenty-seven years, he would soon kill himself, or worse, kill some innocent person with his reckless, drunk driving. She began to pray that things would not go easily for him.

Mark, Josh's father, felt differently. He went to the jail to bail his son out. Then he proceeded to the place where Josh's car had been taken, to bail it out so his son would be able to drive to work the next day. Mark felt that he was doing something right for Josh. Mark feared for his son, that he wouldn't be able to keep up with his work and support his family. To Mark, the worst possible thing was to see Josh go to jail.

What we can glean from these parents is how differently we each respond to fear for our children. Mark wanted to remove the immediate pain from his son; Carol wanted to remove the possibility of worse pain down the road. Mark was seeking to solve Josh's problems for him; Carol was willing to put her son in the hands of God, for Him to deal a severe mercy toward Josh. Mark thought he was doing the Christian thing—showing forgiveness and acceptance for Josh—and he thought his wife was cold and hard because she didn't agree. Carol thought her husband was a sucker and was helping to send their son to an early death by continuing to bail him out.[2]

There are reasons for the variation of how a mother and father respond to their prodigal. Some of the cause is found in the arenas of both personality and gender differences. But during the crisis, who bothers to figure this out?

Have any of the following statements been made to you by your spouse in response to the way you respond to your prodigal? Or have you thought or expressed these to your spouse?

"You seem so hard-hearted."

"Why are you so cold? This is our child. You approach her as if you're a computer."

"You could be more pleasant and friendly when he's around."

"How can you be so heartless? This will drive her further away."

"What you said on the phone seemed so cruel."

The Firm Parent

For the parent who takes the firmer stand, there is more concern for truth than for tact. In the Myers-Briggs Type Indicator, this is a person who makes his decisions in his head rather than his heart. This individual is by nature very logical, detached, analytical. He's motivated by objective values in making decisions. He tends not to become personally involved in a decision and prefers to view the consequence of the action as the main factor. He's seen as firm-minded and tends to critique both ideas and people, as well as see others' flaws. He does recognize people's feelings and emotions as factors to consider, but doesn't place much emphasis on them. Sometimes he ignores the emotional aspects of messages in conversations. His expressions of love are controlled and he demonstrates care quite impersonally. This person is called a *Thinker* since this is his basis for making decisions.

Anyone come to mind as you read this description?

Now consider the other side of the coin with these statements:

"Your heart seems to bleed all over the place for others."

"You're a people-pleaser. You're such a softy you let her walk all over you."

"Why can't you be more logical with this problem? Your feelings get in the way."

"Why don't you use your head instead of your heart?

"I wish you wouldn't take what he does so personally."

The Compassionate Parent

This person referred to in the preceeding statements is more concerned with tact and pleasing than with truth. Decisions are made with the heart rather than the mind. The goal is harmony. She notices when people are hurting and need support. She overlooks negative traits, but appreciates positive ones. She shows concern over the value of different alternatives and how each would affect the people involved. Empathy flows from this person's heart. Expressions of love and concern are frequently expressed. A good decision is one that takes others' feelings into account. This person doesn't want to hurt anyone, even the prodigal. She is concerned about others' feelings and tries to please them, even in unimportant things. She has difficulty giving unpleasant feedback even when it's deserved. According to the Myers-Briggs test, this person is called a *Feeler*, since she make her decisions based on feelings.[3,4]

Mom Versus Dad

Neither of these personality types is right or wrong. Perhaps it's good if one spouse responds from the heart and the other from the head. You both need the perspective of the other approach for balance. If both of you responded from your head, there would be needed elements lacking, and vice versa.

Besides personality differences, gender differences also cause mothers and fathers to respond differently to the prodigal situation.

For example, the majority of men respond to major losses by keeping their thoughts and emotional pain to themselves. If their wife is verbal and a Feeler, it may seem to her that her husband does not care as much as she does. But from the man's perspective, saying little or nothing at all protects him against the vulnerability of having his feelings exposed. Besides, he reasons, why talk about something when there is very little that can be done about it? If the man tends to be silent anyway and is limited in his everyday verbal skills, why would anyone expect him to be any different at this time?

In a major loss, men tend to grieve alone. It's safer to show emotion or express their thoughts when they are by themselves. Unfortunately, men are hampered in the expression of their grief because of cultural expectations, even in today's "enlightened" society. Men are not expected to express loneliness, sadness or depression, helplessness, or to cry openly. Men are supposed to be poised and in control, even when they hear their daughter is pregnant, has AIDS, or is selling drugs as well as herself to support the habit.

Men also want to take physical or legal action over a loss. I've heard men say:

"I'll find that so-and-so that got my son hooked on drugs. I'll turn him in and he'll rot in prison."

"If I find that guy that gave my little girl AIDS, I'll break his neck."

"The school should have been more responsible and strict or none of this would have happened. I'm going to talk to my attorney about this."

"We need to hire a private investigator to find her. I can't believe she ran away with that guy. She wouldn't have done that willingly. The police don't know what they're doing."

Statements like these help a man feel that he is "taking control," which is a major need for him. He also wants something to strike out against, to vent his anger on, and he wants very much to bring about change.

When a man is doing something about his problem, not only does he alleviate the helpless feeling, but he doesn't have to think or feel as much. The more distractions and preoccupations there are, the less a man has to see images in his mind of his prodigal's behavior. He doesn't have to experience the most disturbing feelings. It's a great shut-off mechanism.[5]

Men also have to live up to another image that society puts upon them. During a time of crisis, they are seen as the protector of the other family members. They're supposed to be the pillar of strength that others can lean on. Others view them as being in this role, and whether or not they want to be the leader, they're thrust into or will assume a leadership role at this time. The husband will be looked on as the problem-solver as well as the decision-maker. And because he is fulfilling others' expectations, he may not have the opportunity to adequately deal with his own emotional upset and grief.

Not only is the man expected to make decisions and know what to do—which is difficult in this uncharted territory—but he is also supposed to help serve as the buffer between the painful situation and the rest of the family.[6] This is what a number of fathers said about their situation:

> I wished I'd had some other men to go to—not just to get advice or strength. I didn't need that. I just wanted some other men around that I could be weak in front of . . . you know, just cry and let them know I didn't have the faintest clue of what to do. Maybe one of them had been there before and could tell me it was all right to feel that way.

I wish that others would ask how I was doing once in a while. They're always asking Jean and the kids, but I hurt too. It doesn't feel that this will ever end even though Jimmy's in prison for just two years. It's hard to admit what your child did and where he is. Every time we go to visit, I get sick. I wish I didn't have to go, but then I know he needs us more than ever. I'm just torn in two.

When my daughter told me she was living with him and was pregnant, it's like time stopped. My life seemed to come to a halt. She couldn't be. My wife was more functional than I was and started making plans. I needed to, but wasn't able to. So she got mad at me over that. I didn't have the ability to do anything then. I hurt too much.

Several months later I noticed I was unsure of how to respond to the other three kids. I guess I was blaming myself for what happened and afraid that I'd make a mistake with the others. I knew I needed to be involved and discipline, but if what I did before didn't work, who's to say it will now? I don't want to mess up their lives.

Men struggle with multiple fears that keep them from acknowledging their feelings. Most men fear:
   . . . being vulnerable
   . . . being misunderstood
   . . . inflicting pain on other family members
   . . . losing the respect, admiration, and support of others, especially their peers; losing control of anything in life.

When there are differences, for whatever reason, don't criticize. Use them to compliment each other, and then respond as a team.

Divorced Parents

There is another reason for parents responding differently to their prodigal. We live in a world that contains many fragmented families. It's hard enough for parents to present a united front when they're married and under the same roof. But when divorce occurs, a child ends up living in two worlds. It's easy for parents to be seen as the "good parent" or the "bad parent." Often, one parent is the disciplinarian and the other is more permissive. It is frequently the custodial parent or the one who has the greater amount of time with the child who tends to be the disciplinarian. So it's natural for a child to look forward to spending more time with the lenient parent. This has often been referred to as the "Disneyland Syndrome." When the child goes for his or her weekend visit, the rules are often different or nonexistent. It's playtime, and the child is indulged. It's the perfect way to sabotage the time, energy, and dedication of the custodial parent. I've talked to many who have said it took three or four days for their child to come back down to earth and fit into a normal routine again after one of these visits. Thus, a polarization begins. The child looks forward to escaping from the restrictive home to the permissive one. The protest, "Why do I have to do this? I don't when I'm at their house!" becomes the battle cry.

Now just imagine this scenario played out when the child is a prodigal. Often, by this time, one or both of the original parents have remarried, so there are stepparents and stepsiblings in the picture as well, adding more complications.

Many divorced parents have been caught in a vise when their child starts on the path of a prodigal. For instance, a daughter or son begins smoking or drinking. Their custodial parent says, "No, absolutely not." But the tension builds when the other parent says, "Look. Kids are going to try this stuff. They all do. Just be careful. Don't drink when you're driving. If you have too much to drink, just call me if you need a ride." It's obvious which parent will draw the child. When one parent says no and the other says yes, they end up in competition for the affection of the child.

I've heard the following conflicts numerous times:

"Why can't you be reasonable? Mom lets me bring my girlfriend over to spend the night with me. She knows what's going on. We're going to do it whether she comes over or not. All she says is, 'Be careful and don't make a baby.' You'd see more of me if you'd just lighten up."

"Dad lets me stay out all night, and he's not always questioning me either. He doesn't need to know where I've been. It's a lot more livable being over there."

"Mom lets me bring my friends over anytime. She doesn't have a problem with the way they look. Why should you be so uptight? Maybe I'll just go back and live with her again."

When parents are wrangling for their child's time and attention, it's a struggle to also hang onto their values, especially as the pain increases. It hurts when your child says, "I'd rather be with them. I want to live there." You feel rejected—not just your values, but you personally.

Sometimes there are solutions. Sometimes you just learn to live with the tension and remain faithful to your standards.

It is encouraging when parents pull together, as these surveyed parents did:

To my knowledge my husband and I never seemed to disagree over how to handle situations. There were plenty of times we were both baffled and spent a lot of time brainstorming together. This time of crisis has definitely brought us closer together.

For the most part, we agreed on the course of action. We were in a panic mode, trying anything we could to save our son and the rest of the family.

I can't say enough for my husband's response. He hurt as much as I did but he was always more concerned for how I was doing than his own hurt. He jumped in and helped run the house when I was immobilized. He listened and held me. Most of all though, he supported my hard-line decisions with my daughter. Through this ordeal I discovered that we really did pull together as a team.

My wife was aware of my pain and helped me deal with it. We were both devastated by what our son did and had become, but we realized that we needed to be a team. We talked, debated, and discovered a strength by supporting one another emotionally and spiritually. Knowing that my wife was praying for me and I for her made all the difference in the world.

We discovered the truth of the verse in Ecclesiastes when it says, "Two are better than one, because they have a good return for their work: If one falls down, his friend can help him up. But pity the man who falls and has no one to help him up!" (4:9-10).

Every family is made up of different personalities. Each member is likely to have different views of the prodigal situation and different ideas about how to handle it. Try to respect one another and to value your differences. And above all, don't allow your prodigal to tear down all that is good in your home.

....

1. Don Wegscheider, *If Only My Family Understood Me* (Minneapolis: CompCare, 1979), pp. 35-40, 45-47, adapted.
2. William and Candace Backus, *What Did I Do Wrong?* (Minneapolis: Bethany House Publishers, 1990) pp. 28, 29.
3. Sandra Hirsh and Jean Kummerow, *Life Types* (New York: Warner Books, 1989), pp. 38, 47, adapted.
4. Otto Kroeger and Janet M. Thuesen, *Type Talk* (New York: Tilden Press, A Delta Book, 1988), pp. 18-24, adapted.
5. Carol Staudacher, *Men and Grief* (Oakland: New Harbinger, 1991), pp. 14-38, adapted.
6. Staudacher, pp. 123-126, adapted.

CHAPTER SIX

Responding to Your Child

I once innocently asked a mother and father, "How is your son John?" I was taken aback when they said, "We have no son John." I replied, "But I've met him and talked with him before. I know you have a college-age son by the name of John." They hesitated a bit, and with a sigh said, "Once we had a son. Now we don't because of what he's done. We've disowned him. Most people who ask, we just tell them he died. It's easier and simpler than to explain how he's destroyed his life as well as ours. To us, because of what he did, he died. He's dead. It would have been better if he *had* died!"

Don't Reject . . .

This wasn't just denial of what was happening; it was rejection. It's a temptation for any parent. It's a self-prescribed painkiller against the hurt, shame, and disappointment of having a child rebel.

If you have done this, you may protest, "I'm not really rejecting *him*; I just can't condone what he's doing." But do you really know what the word *reject* means and how we do it?

If you look in the dictionary, you'll find the word means "to cast off" or "to spew out."[1] Some parents do reject their prodigal child this strongly. With or without words, they're saying, "You're no longer a member of this family." It's as though the child has been told, "Don't even use our family name. You're not a member of this family anymore." This is a definite, obvious form of rejection.

Some parents wouldn't go this far. Their rejection is more subtle, less obvious or direct, but it's there all the same. Another definition of the word *reject* is "to refuse to accept or consider." This is the more passive form of rejection that many parents of prodigals employ.

Think about this: *Is there any way in which you've withdrawn from or withheld anything from your relationship with your child?* If so, this is a form of rejection—not of the behavior, but of the child himself or herself.

Sometimes we do this without meaning to, without even realizing this is what we're doing. When you first hear of what your child has done, you're in shock. You're not thinking clearly. You don't know how to respond or what to say, so you may say nothing at all. Some parents persist in this pattern. Withholding communication is a form of rejection. Sometimes rejection occurs when you avoid talking about a specific subject. Many parents have done this. They and the child skirt the problem issue in their discussions or interactions. It's as though they have an unspoken agreement not to talk about the painful area. Perhaps it happens because when they did talk all they did was fight. Nothing was resolved and it always ended up in a painful standoff, so why bring it up again?

I've also seen parents passively reject their prodigal child by withholding encouragement or affirmation. When a child rebels, the action can be so abhorrent to the parents that it blinds them to the positives that still remain in the child's life.

A teenage son who is using drugs may still be getting excellent grades or excelling in sports. Does he hear about this anymore?

A teenage girl who is an accomplished musician is sleeping with her boyfriend. Does she hear about her music, or just the infractions?

An adult son who has announced he is gay continues to rapidly advance in his profession and is honored by the company, his friends, and the community. Is he honored by his parents?

An adult daughter leaves her husband for another man, but continues to provide excellent care and mothering for her children. What does she hear about from her parents?

A son drops out of school to live on the streets because he can't agree with society's values anymore. He helps other street people, but looks and smells like them. What does he hear from his parents?

Many parents are caught up in an "either/or" type of response. They cannot recognize anything good, or positive, as long as the prodigal behavior still exists. I've talked to young adults who, in my eyes, weren't prodigals, but who were rebellious in their parents' eyes.

One young man left seminary after a year because he just didn't feel called to the ministry. He didn't feel that he had wasted the year, because not only had it confirmed that he wasn't called, but he said what he learned would help him be a better layperson in leadership at his church. His parents, however, had always believed he was called to the ministry. They had dedicated him to the ministry at birth and felt God's hand was on him for great things. When he left seminary, they were crushed. His concept of ministry was different than theirs; he wanted to minister to others through counseling. So he went on and earned a Ph.D. in counseling. His friends came to his graduation and celebrated with him. His parents didn't. They never did show any interest in his accomplishments or the number of people he helped. Nor did they ever acknowledge or read any of his five books. Their friends soon learned never to mention their son to them.

Responding in this way, even when the behavior is clearly wrong, is not biblical. Rejection does not bring about a change in the prodigal. It creates a barrier, a wall. It alienates. It's not the path to reconciliation—and we've been called to be reconcilers, not rejecters.[2]

Courage is a quality that parents of rebellious children need desperately. For it will take courage to put into action the ingredients to bring resolution in your relationship with your child. One ingredient is confrontation. In a later chapter you'll read about two others, forgiveness and reconciliation. These three are linked together, but many parents try to bypass one or two of them, which makes any possibility of restoration incomplete.

... Confront!

Confrontation is easy for some, but difficult for others. To some, the word *confront* sounds more like warfare than like a stepping-stone to the healing of a relationship. Confrontation is, simply and essentially, a sharing of facts and feelings. It is not a vindictive attack or an argument. It is not intended to alienate. You don't confront someone for the purpose of releasing your anger against him. In fact, it is best to release your anger *before* a confrontation. You do not confront someone to punish him, get even with him, frighten him, or make him suffer. Rather, confrontation is a way of bringing closure to a painful relationship that would continue to fester if it were not openly discussed and dealt with.

But confrontation does imply correction. Your purpose in confronting is to bring about a correction in the way a person is living her life or handling a relationship. When correction is coupled with caring, the results can be very positive. Your goal in confrontation is not to battle or convict. It's to correct. And there are biblical guidelines for correction.

Correction is meant to be an expression of love. Why put forth the time and energy involved in confrontation if we don't care for the person? Most of the time, correction is painful for one or both of the parties.

It may involve letting your child know that you're aware of what he is doing.

It may involve the placement of some restrictions, if she's living at home.

It may involve asking him to move out, not work for you anymore, turn in his car—especially if he is drinking or using drugs and the car is registered in your name.

It may involve cutting off her funds because of her misuse of them.

Relief for Hurting Parents has twelve excellent examples of how to discipline using natural, or logical, consequences. I'll quote one here, and I encourage you to reference the book for the others:

Children who teach us that they will throw a party in our home when we parents are out of town must no longer be trusted to stay by themselves.

Listen to this letter from one mother to her daughter:

Dear Jane,

I don't blame you for being angry with God, yourself, and even some of your friends. I'll begin by admitting that I'm sure I've made some mistakes as your mom but for all I've done wrong, I must have done something right to end up with such a wonderful daughter. I'm so proud of you.

Someday when you are old enough to understand the logic that motivates a mom, I will tell you:

I loved you enough to ask you about where you were going,

with whom, and request a reasonable time for you to come home.

I loved you enough to encourage you to save money and buy your own bike, stereo system, and phone even though we could have afforded to give them to you.

I loved you enough to forbid you to wear a black leather jacket with long dangling earrings in the sixth grade.

I loved you enough to cancel your twelve-year-old birthday party and made you apologize to Jim and Mrs. Smith for a disrespectful note you had written.

I loved you enough to pray daily that you would desire to live a godly life that was pleasing to yourself, others and, most of all the Lord.

I loved you enough to give you permission to dream and discover your own limits, desires, and goals even if they were different from my own.

I loved you enough to let you see anger, disappointment, disgust, hurt, and tears in my eyes as well as in my heart.

I loved you enough to admit I was wrong (though not often enough) and asked you for your forgiveness.

I loved you enough to stop trying to control your destiny and allowed you to determine your own future even when your choices of self-destruction broke my heart.

I loved you enough to confront you with the truth even when you resented me for it.

I loved you enough to let you experience the natural consequences of your choices even though I ached and my natural instinct was to rescue and protect you from getting hurt.

I loved you enough to let you discover that your newly acquired friends were setting you up for defeat rather than victory.

I loved you enough to give you privileges and then take them away when they were no longer deserved.

But most of all, I loved you enough to say "NO" or "this is wrong and illegal" even when you hated me for it. That was the hardest part of all.

Jane, long ago I gave you to the Lord. I knew you would make choices that would please Him and me and YOU HAVE! I also knew you would make choices that would not be pleasing to Him or to me. I have come to a time and place when I am putting my faith in God, giving you to Him once again as a young adult with a new understanding on my part, that you are accountable to Him and no longer to me. I am free from worry, knowing you are in capable hands.

My love for you is like God's (although it's obviously not as perfect as His) and it will never end. Like God, there will be times I will love you but not love your behavior. I hope you aren't confused and think your performance and accomplishments are tied with my love. There is nothing more you can do to earn my love. No matter what is ahead for us all, my love will never end.

You wouldn't be human if you didn't fail. During my many times of failure I have tried to "get up off the ground, go back to practice the next day, learn from the disappointment, and purpose to break my P.R. at the next meet." I know you can do the same with this recent disappointment and I will be here for you at every turn.

I loved you enough to write this letter,
Mom

The Word of God gives us guidelines for correcting:
"Better is open rebuke than hidden love." (Prov. 27:5)
"Those whom I love I rebuke and discipline." (Rev. 3:19)

When you correct your child, do it in kindness. There is no reason to attack, demean character, or go on and on about what he has done. We can be firm without being angry. We can be direct without putting down. Once it's been said, don't say anymore. When we don't receive a response or acknowledgment from someone, we think we haven't been heard or that our message hasn't registered, so we repeat and we expand. Resist the urge to do that. Your child may need to time to think about and digest what you've said.

It's All in the Approach

When you confront someone, think about what you're hoping to accomplish. Will your manner help you achieve that?

When most people confront, they have expectations of the outcome. It actually works best when your expectations are low, or when you don't expect anything to happen at all. However, if it's a current problem that needs correction, there are some things you can expect—excuses like the following:

- Denial. "Me? You're wrong. I never did that."
- Countercharge. "Yes, but if you hadn't . . ."
- Minimizing. "It's not as bad as you're saying. You're making more of it than it is."
- Ambiguity. "Are you sure you have your facts straight? That's not it at all!"[3]

When you're approaching a trout stream, the way you come up to it can make or break your day. If you stand upright so the sun casts your shadow on the water and if you make noise—don't expect much from the fish. You've spooked them. But if you come up slowly, quietly, carefully, and out of the sun, you have a chance. It's all in your approach.

If you go rushing up to a large dog in its territory, it may think you're an intruder and respond accordingly. But if you stand still, let him come to you and sniff you, he'll probably welcome you into his territory. Again, it's all in the approach.[4]

In the same way, how you approach your child will make a difference. The author of *The Influential Parent* says,

Your approach is like a passport. It allows you to travel outside of your personal world. Once inside someone else's world, you have an opportunity to introduce yourself with an appropriate role and message.[5]

Above all, the way you approach your prodigal needs to be positive so that your child feels positive about herself. Admittedly, this may be a challenge!

David Domico suggests four helpful ways to approach your prodigal.

Be Truthful

First, any approach needs to be *truthful*. There will be times when your child may not appreciate it, but there is really no other option if you want to build trust between you. The way in which truth is expressed, though, is important. Scripture has much to say about it:

Instead, speaking the truth in love, we will in all things grow up into him who is the Head, that is, Christ. (Eph. 4:15)

Therefore each of you must put off falsehood and speak truthfully to his neighbor, for we are all members of one body. (Eph. 4:25)

Do not lie to each other, since you have taken off your old self with its practices. (Col. 3:9)

In light of these passages, how can you best approach your prodigal child? Many parents have said there are two phrases that describe how they feel—"awkward" and "walking on eggshells."

In our hearts, we'll also feel judgment. That's natural. It's normal and it will come as no surprise to your child. What *will* come as a surprise, however, are respect and acceptance. *Don't do what he anticipates.* Remember: be unpredictable. His walls of defense are already erected if he knows what to expect from you. Do the unexpected, and you'll more likely get through.

You're probably thinking, "I can't! There's no way under heaven I can either accept or respect her choice. I can't condone it. I hate what she's chosen." That's true. You don't have to respect or accept her choice in the sense of agreeing with it. I probably wouldn't either. But you *can* respect and accept her as a person, especially when you remind yourself how much God loves and values her.

He doesn't have to agree with your values or even the Bible's values for you to respect and accept him. We have to continually remind ourselves how much Jesus loved and respected the worst of the lot!

Don't be afraid to tell her how you feel. And don't be concerned if you hear statements such as:

"There you go again."

"I know what you believe. You've drilled it into me for years."

"Don't lecture me. Can't you accept me for who I am? God created me this way."

Your child may be defensive. This is probably nothing new to you. Let him be. You can't change it. You *can* let him know that you're going to share how you feel and why—once, and that's all. Don't go over it again and again and again. Don't leave books open or send him anonymous articles. He'll know where they came from and tune you out even more. And remember, the way you say it is important. Angry yelling or caustic, digging comments have no place. They damage and push away rather than resolve. Those things reinforce his behavior. However, during this time it's all right to call your child's behavior what you feel it is—a mistake, a sin, a risk, unwise, disappointing, etc. Use phrases like "I feel

...," or "From my perspective . . . ," rather than, "You are . . . ." She needs to know that, even though you don't approve of what she's doing, you do love and accept her. Don't be surprised, though, when she responds with, "What I do is who I am. It's me. If you really accept me, you'd accept what I do."[6]

Be Tender

The second approach is to be *tender*. Everyone, including your child, needs to hear soft statements of concern. It reflects sensitivity and tolerance, as well as nurturing.

Be Unarmed

The third approach is quite different. Have you ever considered *approaching your prodigal unarmed?* Strange question, but consider it for a moment. We all have our arsenal of weapons that we employ in relationships. Often, we approach our child with our weapons ready to fire, as if we were daring him to react in a certain way that we won't like. Sometimes our expectations are a self-fulfilling prophecy, since he picks up on the fact that our arsenal is armed and our finger is on the hair trigger.

If you approach unarmed, you're open to hear what is said, to consider it, to keep communication positive—and your approach will probably disarm your child as well. Remember this: *You will have more influence and control when you approach unarmed rather than armed.*

If your child tends to respond in an attacking manner, where did she learn this approach? If she is defensive, where did she learn this?

Who in your family approaches others with the biggest arsenal of weapons? What does this accomplish? How do others respond to this? It's something to think about.

Be Reasonable

The last approach is the *reasonable* approach. Has your child or teen ever said, "Mom. Dad. Come on. Be reasonable." What is he asking for? Could it be fairness? Calmness? Openness? When your child is angry or upset, the tender approach is better than the reasonable. When emotional energy subsides, the reasonable works better.[7] This approach is best described by the author of *The Influential Parent:*

> Being reasonable does not mean being so objective that you eliminate empathy or a caring attitude. In this approach, you are

working to stay open-minded to issues that may trigger strong feelings of resistance. This may involve extra work on your part. At times a parent using this approach might say, "My initial reaction is to say no. That's because what you want to do makes me feel afraid for your safety. I need some time to sort out my feelings before we talk about this rationally. Otherwise I'm likely to say no without hearing you out completely." You may have to postpone a decision on something at a time when your child wants an immediate response. You may have to collect your thoughts before engaging your child in an emotional conversation. You may have to talk with someone else in order to sort out your feelings. You may have to listen to all of what they have to say before drawing a conclusion. A reasonable approach is one in which you are informed by your feelings but not controlled by them to the point that you become rigid and unyielding. In this approach there is always room for an appeal.[8]

Expect your prodigal to want her own way. She believes she's right and entitled to what she asks or demands. So . . . which is easier for you to say . . . yes or no? Think back.

Did you ever struggle with saying no to your children when they were preschoolers? In grade school? Adolescents? If so, you'll probably have the same problem saying the "N" word when they're adults as well. When a child of any age is in difficulty, we tend to shut down, tune out, and react. Instead, we should follow the LTDP Approach.

Use the LTDP Approach

First of all, the L in LTDP means *Listen.* Hear your child out. Focus on both words and feelings. Look for the message beneath the message. Often, what is said may not be the real issue. Listen for what he has difficulty putting into words. You may hear what you don't want to hear or agree with. That's all right. *At least he's talking.* If you give yourself permission to hear what you don't want to, you'll handle it much better. Remember that listening means that you're not thinking about what you're going to say when the other person stops talking. It also means you're not judging what or how he's saying it. Remember Proverbs 18:13: "He who answers a matter before he hears the facts, it is folly and shame to him" (AMP).

The T stands for *Think.* Decisions made without thinking usually backfire. When your child makes a request, you have three choices:

You could say yes immediately. This is unwise.

You could react toward her with a statement of shock and unbelief for even considering such a request. This, too, is unwise, since it's inflammatory and could shut the door on continuing discussion.

You could say "Let me (or us) think about it. We need some time. When do you need to know?" The only way you can evaluate the matter is to give yourself time. Remember these guidelines from Proverbs:

> He who foams up quickly and flies into a passion will deal foolishly, and a man of wicked plots and plans is hated. (Prov. 14:17, AMP)

> He who is slow to anger has great understanding, but he who is hasty of spirit exposes and exalts his folly. (Prov. 14:29, AMP)

> A fool's wrath is quickly and openly known; but a prudent man ignores an insult. . . . There are those who speak rashly like the piercing of a sword, but the tongue of the wise brings healing. (Prov. 12:16, 18, AMP)

> He who guards his mouth keeps his life, but he who opens wide his lips will come to ruin. (Prov. 13:3, AMP)

The D is for *Discuss*. If you're married, talk the matter over with your spouse. If not, use a trusted friend. Gaining the advice and wisdom of others is essential. Someone else may have greater objectivity and a better perspective than you do at this time.

The P is for *Pray*. The best place to gain wisdom is at the feet of the Lord. You need to pray for the wisdom to make the right decision.

One couple was facing a request from an adult son that seemed to have some merit, but they weren't certain. They prayed about it separately each morning and then together each evening for two weeks. They also created a list with two columns: "reasons we should do this" and "reasons we should not." It helped them make what they thought was the right decision.[9]

There are good ways to say no and there are the other ways that are too easy to use, especially when we're upset.

Being reasonable is a positive approach. Answers need to be accompanied with good reasons (that make sense to you).

Being reasonable doesn't mean your child will like your response or will agree with it. It does mean that you've thought it through and this is the best wisdom you have at this point. Being gentle as well as reasonable helps the other person not to become inflamed. There is tenderness and compassion in this kind of approach.

To summarize so far—remember,

- We're *not* to reject
- We *are* to confront
- We are to be open and honest
- It is all right to say no.

Accept and Encourage

But the next two principles may be more difficult:

1. Accept your child.
2. Encourage your child.

Accepting and encouraging are part of our calling as believers *whether we want to or not*. We are called to communicate with our child, encourage him, show affection, and give emotional support, interest, and affirmation. Margie Lewis says:

Genuine, aggressive acceptance needs to be expressed in such clear words and acted out in such open-armed fashion that it can't possibly be misunderstood. It must be so obvious, so overwhelming that it sets our children at ease by overcoming the disease that exists because of our differences and because of such feelings as guilt and regret.[10]

She goes on to tell this story:

Another illustration of this kind of unmistakable acceptance was shared with me by a Christian mother whose son is living with his girlfriend. "When Alex came home to tell us he'd moved in with Claudia, I burst into tears, even though I'd halfway expected it for months," Bonnie Ahrens said. "I told him we could never approve, but of course he knew that. I also told him because he was our son we would keep loving him no matter what.

"But accepting the girl was impossible as far as I was concerned," Bonnie continued. "I didn't even want to talk to her. But when I expressed my feelings to my own daughter, she said, 'Mom, it's very possible she and Alex will get married someday. And if that happens I want to like and get along with my sister-in-law.'

"That started me thinking," Bonnie said. "I determined to get my relationship with my son's girlfriend off on the right foot. And I began to look for ways to show my acceptance of her.

"Christmas promised to be an awkward time. But when I learned Alex wanted to bring Claudia over to our house for our family celebration, I decided to make her feel welcome. We spent as much money on gifts for her as we did for our own daughter.

"We had a beautiful Christmas day together as a family. We were all able to relax and enjoy what I had feared might be a strained experience. I know my feelings were accurate because as Alex and Claudia said their good-byes at the door, Claudia gave my husband an impulsive hug. Then she came to me and gave me a hug.

"As I put my arms around her to squeeze back, my emotions welled up inside me. I didn't want to let go. But when I did and when they were gone, I tried to analyze my feelings. It was as if my deliberate acts of acceptance, the sharing of a Christmas meal, the giving of gifts, had released in me a surge of loving acceptance. For the first time I was really able to care about Claudia.

"Not long after that Claudia said to me, 'Your family is so close. I wish my family could be like that.' Then I knew our attitude of acceptance was making an impression, not only on her, but on our son, Alex."

Acceptance has a way of doing that. Where rejection only creates resistance, acceptance softens, melts, bridges, and soothes. Many other hurting parents I've talked to echo Bruce Crane's feeling that "acceptance has been the single most important factor through which God seemed to work." And a number of hurting parents' sons or daughters who have since turned to God and the faith of their parents have told me, "Their acceptance kept the channels open and made me want to hold on to my family."[11]

One of the best ways to demonstrate acceptance is by encouragement. Do you understand what this word means?

To be an encourager you need to have an attitude of optimism. The *American Heritage Dictionary* has one of the better definitions of the word. It says encouragement is a "tendency or disposition to expect the best possible outcome, or to dwell on the most hopeful aspect of a situation." When this is your attitude or perspective, you'll be able to encourage your child. Encouragement is "to inspire; to continue on a chosen course; to impart courage or confidence." It has to occur, not because of, but in spite of what your child has done or how you feel.

Encouragement is sometimes thought of as praise and reinforcement, but it's also much more than that. Praise is limited. It's a verbal reward. It emphasizes competition, has to be earned, and is often given for being the best. *Encouragement is freely given.* It can involve noticing what others take for granted and affirming something others notice but may never think of mentioning.

Consider what God's Word says about this:

In Acts 18:27, the word *encourage* means "to urge forward or persuade." In 1 Thessalonians 5:11, it means "to stimulate another person to the ordinary duties of life."

First Thessalonians 5:14 (AMP) says, "And we earnestly beseech you, brethren, admonish (warn and seriously advise) those who are out of line—the loafers, the disorderly and the unruly; encourage the timid and fainthearted, help and give your support to the weak souls [and] be very patient with everybody—always keeping your temper."

Scripture uses a variety of words to describe both our involvement with others as well as the actual relationship. "Urge" (*parakaleo*) means "to beseech or exhort." It is intended to create an environment of urgency to listen and respond to a directive. It is a mildly active verb. Paul used it in Romans 12:1 and in 1 Corinthians 1:4.

The word translated "encourage" (*paramutheomai*) means "to console, comfort, and cheer up." This process includes elements of understanding, redirecting of thoughts, and a general shifting of focus from the negative to the positive. In the context of the verse, it refers to the timid ("fainthearted" in KJV) individual who is discouraged and ready to give up. It's a matter of loaning your faith and hope to the person until his own develops.

Help *(anechomai)* primarily contains the idea of "taking interest in, being devoted to, rendering assistance, or holding up spiritually and emotionally." It is not so much an active involvement as a passive approach. It suggests the idea of coming alongside a person and support-ing him. In the context of 1 Thessalonians 5:14, it seems to refer to those who are incapable of helping themselves.

First Thessalonians 5:11 states, "Therefore encourage one another and build each other up, just as in fact you are doing."

Hebrews 3:13 says we're to "encourage one another every day." In the setting of this verse, encouragement is associated with protecting the believer from callousness.

Hebrews 10:25 says, "Let us encourage one another." This time the word means to keep someone on his feet who, if left to himself, would collapse. Your encouragement serves like the concrete pilings of a structural support.

Which of these passages is needed at this time in the life of your child? You might have a tendency to concentrate on the word "admonish" in 1 Thessalonians. But your child has probably already been warned and advised, by you and perhaps by others. Now is the time to let the Holy Spirit do the warning and advising.

In what way does your child need to be encouraged? What can you say or do that will provide that encouragement?

....

1. *Webster's New World Dictionary*, Third Edition, (New York: Simon and Schuster), 1994, p. 1,132.
2. Margie M. Lewis with Gregg Lewis, *The Hurting Parent* (Grand Rapids, Mich.: Zondervan, 1988), pp. 56-59, adapted.
3. David Stoop and James Masteller, *Forgiving Our Parents, Forgiving Ourselves* (Ann Arbor, Mich.: Servant Publications, 1991), p. 276-277, adapted.
4. David Domico, *The Influential Parent* (Wheaton, Ill.: Shaw Publishers, 1997), p. 143.
5. Domico, p. 143.
6. William Coleman, *How to Go Home Without Feeling Like a Child* (Dallas: Word Publishing, 1991), p. 72, adapted.
7. Coleman, pp. 148-152, adapted.
8. Domico, p. 152.
9. Stephen A. Bly, *Just Because They've Left, Doesn't Mean They're Gone* (Colorado Springs: Focus on the Family, 1993) pp. 88-92, adapted.
10. Lewis, pp. 72-73.
11. Lewis, pp. 73-74.

CHAPTER SEVEN

Decisions, Decisions

Every parent's life is full of decisions regarding their children. When the children are young, you make every decision for them—what to eat, what to wear, when to sleep. As they grow older, you begin to relax a bit, allowing them more and more choices as they mature and develop. And when they're launched into adulthood . . . what a relief!

Unless, that is, your child is a prodigal. With Sheryl, once we had gotten through the teenage years, we thought we were home free—but it wasn't to be. Instead of sitting back and enjoying the fruits of our labor, we were plunged back into the decision-making mode. But this time, each decision was weighted with the attachment of a moral dilemma.

What decisions are you facing with regard to your prodigal child? Most of the time, there are no easy solutions. Many parents have found it helpful to clarify and identify what they're facing in writing. Perhaps some of the following issues will hit home for you:

Should I try to force my grown child to go into treatment when he doesn't want it?

Who pays for a treatment program? Do I? How many times?

How important are my own needs by comparison?

Should I insist on a Christian treatment program?

Should I let the law deal with my child's illegal behavior, or should I try to intervene to protect my child from punishment? How do I best help my child?

Should I call the police and have my own child arrested, or should I try to handle him myself even if he seems dangerous?

Should I speak up on topics I know will offend him if I think they're important?

Should I be kind and receptive to his friends even if their behavior often offends my morals and values? Or should I risk driving my child away by offending his friends?

Should I allow him to bring his lover, male or female, home for a visit? If so, should I forbid them to sleep together under my roof? What if they're upset with my "Puritanism"?

Should I arrange to have my older child deprogrammed to get him out of a weird, non-Christian cult? Or should I keep my hands off and just pray?

Should I let myself love and get attached to my daughter's out-of-wedlock baby? Will I be condoning her lifestyle if I seem to enjoy the little one?

Should I continue to give him money when he is capable of earning his own but won't hold a job?

Should I give him money when he uses it frivolously and keeps wanting more?

Should I allow my grown child to move home because he wants to save on rent money?

What can I do if my adult child never gets around to moving to his own quarters even though he is old enough to be on his own?

Should I provide contraceptives for my seventeen-year-old daughter when she tells me she's sleeping around?

How do I know when I can trust a child who has often broken trust with me?

My child is getting a divorce, but my sympathies are with the spouse, who is not even my own child. What should I do? What should I say?[1]

I've heard parents say, "How do I know I made the right decisions when the kids were growing up? How do I know I'm responding the best way now?" Maybe you haven't been the perfect parent. In fact, I'm sure you haven't been—none of us is! But at this moment, it doesn't matter what you did before. It's what you do now that's important. You can let this crisis serve as a wake-up call in your relationship with your child and eradicate any unhealthy patterns you have allowed to develop.

Roles Parents Play

In order to do that, let's identify some of the risky roles parents tend to fall into.

The Pleaser

First, let's take the *pleaser.* Consider the following questions:

Do you anticipate and try to meet the needs of your adult child without checking with her first?

Do you have a strong need for this child's approval?

Do you defer your own need fulfillment or preferences in order to please this child? (If so, chances are good it's not fully appreciated, perhaps not even noticed).

Do you spend more time, money, and emotional energy on this older teen or adult child than on yourself?

Do you feel responsible to make sure this child you're concerned about is not deprived in any way?

If you are a pleaser, it is unlikely that you function in this role only with your child. It's difficult to let go of this way of life because it feels so "nice," even "Christian." But pleasing is actually not good—not for you, and not even for the other person. It doesn't allow her to grow up, to become responsible. And if your emotional well-being depends on her being happy with you, you have placed an intolerable burden on her shoulders that she will not want to bear for long.

This is an area that needs to be transformed by the renewing of your mind (see Eph. 4:23). Stop yourself when you are tempted to answer in a pleasing way. When your prodigal child makes a request, tell him you need time to think before you give him your decision. And when your decision is no, that's all you have to say. You're not obligated to give your reasons. It's all right if he doesn't care for your answer—after a lifetime of your giving in to him, he's bound to resist a change! But you don't need his approval. You already have God's approval. Use your common sense.

"He grants good sense to the godly—His saints. . . . He shows how to distinguish right from wrong, how to find the right decision every time." (Prov. 2:7-9, TLB)

The Rescuer

Next, let's look at the *rescuer*. How can you tell if you're a rescuer? Think about these questions:

Do you tend to feel more "loving" toward your child when he needs you to bail him out?

Do you feel it's your duty to take care of whatever your child can't handle?

Do you feel guilty if your child needs help and you don't give it?

At some level, do you find that you privately welcome an opportunity to rescue your child because it helps you to keep or win her affection? Is there a part of you that fears losing her love?

If you answered yes to these questions, you are most likely a rescuer.

But does your child really need rescuing? Think of it this way. If you weren't alive, wouldn't your child find a way to survive? Sure, it may be hard, and he might have to delay gratification for awhile, but that's what life is all about. *Rescuing a child at any age retards his emotional development.* It keeps him a perpetual child.

Is it possible that you are using rescuing this child as a means to avoid confronting your own personal issues? If you weren't using your time and energy on this child, what would you focus on in your own life? When we take on the responsibility to rescue, we exclude God from the equation—in our own life as well as our child's.

Whose pain are you more sensitive to at this time—yours, or your child's?

When do you feel best about yourself as a parent—when you rescue or when you don't?

Your answers tell a story.

The Victim

Another role that a parent can assume is that of *victim*. Some people truly are victims because of tragedies they've experienced in their lives. My friend Rich Buhler has written and lectured extensively on this subject. In his book *Pain and Pretending* he defines *victim* in this way:

A victim is a person who has experienced destruction at the foundation of who that person is and in a way that has caused significant hindrance in the living of life.[2]

Think through these questions for a moment to see if they describe the way you feel.

Do you often feel overwhelmed by life or by other people, including your child?

Do you feel unsafe most of the time, and is it difficult to trust others?

Do you prefer being alone rather than being with others? Not because of your personality, but because being with people makes you feel fearful or worried.

Do you feel a sense of alienation from your children, or do you see yourself as a burden to them, even though they have never indicated feeling that way?

Do you have the feeling that nothing ever works out for you and others get all the breaks?

How is your energy level? Do you feel tired most of the time? Is it possible that you live with a low-grade depression related to your life experiences or relationships? (For assistance in this area see my book *Winning Over Your Emotions*).

Do you have difficulty focusing on simple, everyday tasks?

Do you rely inappropriately on food, money, prescriptions, or any substances to help you feel better?

If you identified with these questions, it is likely that you see yourself, consciously or subconsciously, as a victim. Perhaps you have had a history of being victimized in some way, or perhaps your current circumstances make you feel that way. Either way, it may be necessary to confront this issue in your own life before a productive relationship can be built with your child. If you function as a victim, you can expect difficulties in communication, confrontation, intimacy, and even spiritual growth. In this world of ours, there are many victims of abuse and violence, and there are many who have experienced trauma in their lives. But there is a difference between being victimized by an act or acts and living as a perpetual victim. Many parents feel destroyed by what their child has done. That's a natural response. But it needn't define your life.

The Manipulator

The next role to consider is that of *manipulator*. Manipulating is an easy pattern to fall into, especially when you feel little control over your child's behavior or choices—but it isn't effective. In fact, it makes things worse. Karen O'Connor describes the cycle:

Parents who don't get their way with a few well-chosen words usually escalate their tactics. They use repetition, silence, anger, verbal abuse, and brooding to wear down their opponent. Some even stoop to bribes. They give or withhold monetary and other rewards if they don't succeed.

After an encounter with such parents, adult children are worn down and exhausted. They feel frustrated, furious, and futile over the lack of respect they receive. Some vow never again to put themselves in a situation like this. Sometimes weeks, months, even years go by without contact. Manipulative parents overwhelm and adult child victims feel too vulnerable in their presence—so they withdraw rather than subject themselves to this mistreatment.[3]

How do you know if you tend to be a manipulator? Consider these questions.

Do you have difficulty expressing your needs and desires directly?

Do you use guilt and shame to motivate your adult child? Do you ever bring up the past to motivate your adult child?

Do you blame your child for your own difficulties?

Do you avoid a direct confrontation with your difficult child because you are afraid of her disapproval?

Do you have difficulty expressing your feelings honestly and directly?

Do you feel guilty and angry because your child has rejected your values?

Do you believe your child owes you respect?

Do you tend to dwell on the past and struggle to live in the present?[4]

Karen O'Connor, in her helpful book *Restoring Relationships with Your Adult Children,* offers some biblical help for breaking out of the nonproductive parenting roles we sometimes feel stuck in:

Now choose life, so that you and your children may live and that you may love the Lord your God, listen to his voice, and hold fast to him. (Deut. 30:19-20)

What does it mean to "choose" life? I believe it means that we are to intentionally line up with God as we know and understand Him. He is the God of life—life here on earth and life everlasting. Choosing life may include for you, turning your will and your life over to His care in a conscious way, seeking Him through prayer and meditation, listening for His guidance for your behavior, and holding onto Him as a small child would hold onto a loving parent. It may include letting go of your expectations, your way of doing things, your agenda for yourself and your adult children, and discovering what God has for each of you.[5]

Enabling Versus Tough Love

Eliminating unhealthy ways of relating is a big first step to a better relationship with your prodigal. But that isn't an overnight process, and in the meantime, you may still need to proceed on a course of action. Let's take a moment to define a couple of terms. Understanding them will help you establish a foundation for good decision-making.

This first term is *enabling*. It arose from alcohol and drug-addiction treatment programs, but in this context, an enabler is a person who, by wanting to help, actually makes it easier for a prodigal to continue his destructive behavior.

Some parents enable in a direct way, by actually obtaining the alcohol or drugs, etc., for their child, or by providing money for such. Others enable in indirect ways, perhaps by making excuses to their child's employer, doing his work for him, or covering up for him in other ways. Here's how Buddy Scott describes it:

> If you help your children get away with doing wrong by helping them get by with it, you are actually helping them do wrong. *You are enabling them to continue to do wrong* apart from the impact of bad consequences. Your help is putting off their realizing how badly they need to change. Changing doesn't have to be important to them because somehow, some way, everything turns out okay; they see no need to change!
>
> You are getting in the way of cause and effect, in the way of nature running its course. Your difficult child is not experiencing the potholes in the road of hard knocks if you are letting him or her walk on you instead of on the road itself!
>
> One of the most effective teachers is the road of hard knocks.

For *good*ness sake, you must let this stern substitute teacher—
natural consequences—teach your children. This teacher is for
those kids who refuse to learn by listening to their parents, teachers, and church leaders. They relegate themselves to learn by
experience.

Parents can unwittingly become a part of their teenagers'
successful-system-for-doing-wrong-and-getting-by-with-it.
Their kids turn them into their safety net. They know that if they
get into serious trouble, their parents will always be there to
"catch" them—to talk to school officials, to pay their fines, or to
get them out of jail.[6]

In short, *enabling* means helping another person to act in an irresponsible way and get away with it.

There is only one solution to enabling: immediately withdrawing all
types of support, direct and indirect, that make the prodigal child's
destructive behavior possible. Love takes action for the welfare of a child;
it doesn't assist the child to do worse. Letting an older teen or adult stay
in your house while continuing a destructive lifestyle doesn't make sense.

Conflicts between parents and their children may sometimes
demand immediate parental action. Grim moments in family life
arise when parents feel that they must make a stand. Such confronta-
tions often occur when an adult is still dependent upon financial
support—or still living at home. Parents who rightly demand that in
their own home their own moral standards of acceptable behavior be
observed may find their guidelines constantly ignored. When an
adult child refuses to work, go to school, seek therapy, or conform to
family standards of conduct, parents can feel mounting anger and
anxiety. Why is this young adult collapsing back into this childlike
dependency and self-destructive rebellious behavior? Should I
demand that he leave the house?

Parents can feel paralyzed and helpless. Habits of going the
second mile and generations of a family's heritage of loyalty and
commitment to one's kin make the thought of ousting one's own
flesh and blood a hard step to take. If in the turmoil a mother and
father disagree about what to do, a stalemate can ensue. Often
parents swing back and forth between making demands and
setting rules for better behavior, and when that fails, backing

down and continuing to provide support.

Parents faced with adult children who are engaging in seriously troubled and offensive behavior have a problem in discerning what is happening. Is this adult child seriously neurotic, chemically addicted, or somehow mentally impaired? Or is this a person capable of self-sufficiency but refusing to make the effort? When one determines the child is unimpaired and is capable of acting in a responsible grown-up way, it is time to act.[7]

The second term is *tough love*. It's the refusal to help the prodigal child continue to be irresponsible or to allow yourself to be victimized. This is an approach of demanding mature, responsible behavior, even if it means cutting off contact until the child changes. (This approach is most appropriate in cases of alcohol or drug use or abuse at home; it is not generally effective with a child who is in a cult, living with her partner, etc.) It isn't easy standing by watching a child self-destruct—and it isn't always the right thing to do. Each parent has to decide when and how to implement this approach.

With both of these terms, the main principle is to be sure you don't do anything that helps the prodigal perpetuate his rebellious lifestyle—and that you takes steps to make his bad choices as uncomfortable as possible. Remember the father in Luke 15? His joyful response and showering of love came *after* his son had changed his lifestyle. He didn't send money to the faraway country to help his son live it up with harlots. He let his son sink to the pigpen and find out about the realities of life.[8]

Since one of the most common prodigal problems is drug use, let's take an extra moment to read as Buddy Scott elaborates on this specific situation:

> You may think you are doing the right thing by shielding your children, but you must recognize this extremely important fact: The stuff kids can get into today can turn out their lights forever! Drugs can blow their mental circuits beyond repair. Certain diseases that they might catch can injure them permanently (like genital herpes) or even kill them (like AIDS). Their offspring can be born afflicted due to genetic damage from drugs, or they can be born with AIDS. *It is urgent* that self-destructive teenagers come face-to-face with how wrong their wrong is just as soon as possible![9]

As soon as you discover that your child's life has begun to revolve around life-threatening problems, you can say . . .

We won't house, feed, or clothe you (we won't give you a stable base of operation) so that you can keep on destroying yourself. We will not continue to produce for you while you use our supplies to help you and your friends destroy you. We will always help you up, but we will never keep you up while you are going down.

Drug abusers get with the drug crowd and stay at it for so long that they become physically and economically exhausted. Then they bring their pitiful-looking remains home to their parents and promise to change (and they are probably sincere at the time).

Their parents' hopes soar, and they take them in and nurse them back to health. But these abused parents don't know that their children are just vacationing with them from doing drugs. More often than not, they'll go back to it as soon as they're up to it again (because they almost never can change by themselves, no matter how good their intentions are).

That is why, in most cases, I urge parents to make the rule that their children can return home only through a drug treatment program. Providing transportation to a treatment program can be the parents' most effective response to the drug-dependent person who is requesting help.

Although tough love is critical when dealing with substance abuse, it can be effective, even necessary, for other problems as well. We asked the parents we surveyed whether they had practiced tough love. These are some of their responses:

When it was obvious there was alcohol and drug use by our teen, we drew lines that said such use would not be accepted in our home. We recognized that she would do what she wanted to do but, if discovered, there would be consequences. We felt those boundaries were in her best interest and for her safety, to say nothing about lawful. Her father (who lived elsewhere), on the other hand, understood that kids engaged in such activities and was concerned she remain safe. He desired that she call if she needed a ride home or needed to sleep over somewhere due to intoxication. We desired to know where she was and with whom and didn't allow overnight activities that involved both males and females. The activities that were allowed from the other household were much less restrictive. We still believe that we provided what she needed, not necessarily what she wanted; however, it had a great price tag. The hatred and rejection from her had to be accepted in order to do what we believed was the right thing and the most loving thing.

We still are practicing tough love. It is hard to do sometimes because we would love to have a whole healthy family. We refuse, however, to pay her insurance, health or car, fund her lifestyle, pay her bills, or even her college. We did help with all these things until she decided she would rather live with her boyfriend. We are allowing her to get sick of living and eating out of the pig's trough.

Allowing our gay son to call us with details of his sex life was like allowing him to dump his dirty ashtray all over the living room carpet. We had to set boundaries concerning what topics we were willing to discuss with him. Expressing our unconditional love for him without condoning his lifestyle was difficult. Both my husband and I agreed we needed to ask the Holy Spirit to give us the "God" kind of love that put our feelings subservient to praying for his restoration.

I did practice tough love and grace. My behavior might or might not be always right. But when my daughter was in college, I did ask her opinion. She told me she needed to hear "NO!" She needed to see me follow [my decisions] with punishment (consequences). I was too soft and she felt insecure. She also told me my love and concern *did* help her not get into bigger trouble. I guess they can feel and realize our motivation, love, and forgiveness. I felt like I was trying to save a big fire from burning my child. I was also surprised at my forgiveness towards her. The love looked like God the Father's unconditional forgiveness and acceptance towards the Prodigal Son. He welcomed him home.

We kicked our daughter out and refused to supply anything until she agreed to negotiate with our team. We tried our best to make sure she knew the reason we were doing this. Unfortunately, she has become extremely self-centered and always tries to put blame on others, and tries to send us on a guilt trip.

I thought we had instituted tough love when our prodigal moved back in with us. We sat down and drew up a contract between her and us that we felt was fair and equitable. We all signed it. However, the prodigal never kept the things on the contract. My husband felt it was no big deal and the important thing was that she stayed in school. The contract became of no effect.

I don't know how to love a person that has nearly destroyed what I thought was good in my life. I have always been raised to think you hate the sin and love the sinner, but I'm finding it hard to love someone when they continue to victimize you and have no desire to have any relationship with you.

As a measure of tough love, after my daughter ran away, I completely stripped her bedroom and carefully packed all of her things away in boxes and stored them in the attic above the garage. If she tried to get into our house, I wanted her to see that things were not the same as before. I wanted her to see that she could not manipulate us and make our home as a revolving door. Sure enough, on her sixteenth birthday, I came home to find she and a couple friends had broken into our house through a bathroom window. She was carrying out her skis, which were about the only items left in her bedroom. The fact that this was midsummer, and that as a runaway she expected to support a lifestyle that included skiing, made a rather incongruous scene. She was furious and shocked. A few days later, she asked to be given her things. We complied, feeling it was only just to do so, but asked her to make an appointment to come collect them.

The parenting group we attend is a bit similar to a tough love group. After struggling through the first few months of trying to erase the problem we realized it wasn't working. Our son was pushing and stretching every boundary we set. We even came to the point where we couldn't see how he could continue to live with us. I think that was the peak of the anger for each of us, him and us. We realized that we needed help and sought it, and he seemed to realize if he didn't try he would have to leave. When he was charged for theft we realized that he needed a wake-up call. We insisted he be charged even though he returned the stolen goods. My husband went to court with him, cried with him, but we felt he needed to be accountable for all we had tried to teach him, etc. Through it all we continued to tell him we loved him and wanted him in our home; however, we wouldn't stand by and watch him destroy himself by using drugs, etc. We have stuck by this, even though at times it has been so tough. Our son has moved ahead in a lot of ways. We can see many positive changes as he matures slowly; however, he has had his share of setbacks as well. When they come, we have learned to let the chips fall, to not always rush in and try to make it easier, etc. If he breaks curfew, we ensure he tells his probation officer. When he slips on his drug use (one of the terms of his probation is to be drug-free), we ensure he tells her. He decided he needed a monthly drug test to help himself to stay clean and, PTL, he is presently drug-free. We do realize that whether he stays that way or not will remain in his control. He recently got a job, which can be a good thing as long as he uses his money for the right things, but again we realize that this is in his control. I have learned to be a more grateful person through all this. God extends us such grace . . . we know we need to model that to him now more than ever. I read somewhere that whoever values the child the most will win that child . . . we fully intend to value our son the most!

Yes, we did practice tough love, grace, boundaries, and everything else we could think of. Nothing worked until I started having support group meetings in my home with a local Christian police officer who wanted to do something about all of the teens on drugs in our community. I eventually turned over some drugs I found in my daughter's purse to him to analyze. He called back to confirm that it was methamphetamine and he was on his way over to arrest her. I could not do anything to stop this from happening. I thought he was just going to tell me what it was and then I could do something about it. But that was not the case. He came over with another officer and it really scared her. They did not take her in but she had to go to court and pay a large fine. That was the beginning of the end of her drug use. She was really scared and knew we would not put up with it anymore. This particular drug causes violent behavior and very bad mood swings. My daughter was nothing like I knew her to be, so loving her was extremely difficult. She was not a mother to her son and only seemed to care about herself. I prayed a lot and had to let her go for safety sake. I really didn't like her most of the time.

Rescuing Versus Helping

One of the hardest things for many parents to do is to stand firm. They go back and forth, questioning the wisdom of the stance they've taken. Too often, this results in yet another rescue disguised as help. How can you know when you're rescuing rather than helping? Consider these guidelines:

- How often do you find yourself canceling your own plans to do what your older child claims he needs you to do? It is reasonable to do this once in a great while, but it should not happen regularly.
- Have you allowed your grown child to come live with you even when she could live elsewhere—even when you really don't want her staying in your home?
- How often have you "loaned" your child money and never had it repaid? It might be interesting to make a list of your child's debts to you. Unusual circumstances can make this understandable, but few things short of natural disasters should make it a regular occurrence.
- Have you been tempted to find some way to make life easier for your child, hoping that it will help him get his life straightened out? An easy life seldom motivates anyone to do what he needs to do.

What if your child now has a child of her own? She may use this to get to you. You feel trapped into helping, and your child uses this to manipulate you. Listen to what other grandparents have said:

They'd take our granddaughter right into the drug party if we didn't baby-sit her for them.

We pay their rent because if we didn't they'd have to live with a bunch of other lowlifes and no telling what our grandbaby would be exposed to.

Sure we get him out of jail. If he stays in jail, he'll lose his job, and then how will they provide for the baby?

We've lost a son; we can't stand the thought of losing a grandson. The only spiritual training he gets is when he's with us. We've just got to stay close to them.

We know they're using us, but that's the only way we get to help with the grandbaby.

Helplessness is not a pretty sight, especially in a grown child. Sometimes we inadvertently perpetuate this by treating him as if he really can't get along without us. There is a season of dependence in the life of every child. But to become an adult, he must shift to independence, even if he doesn't show signs of moving this direction on his own. Parents need to step out of the way, even if the child falls flat on his face at times.

When eagles raise a young eaglet, they take care of it for months, bringing it food and meeting all its needs. The day comes, however, when they literally kick it out of the nest. It either flies or crashes. If the parents swooped down underneath the young bird to catch it, it would never learn to flap and strengthen its own wings. Eventually it would die.

Passive Parenting Versus Active Parenting

Are you behaving like an eagle? Or are you more concerned with spreading a safety net beneath your young? It is helpful to understand that there are two styles of parenting: *passive* parenting and *active* parenting. It's not that one is good and the other bad; actually, we all use both styles. Passive parenting is in effect almost constantly, as we privately observe or wonder about what's occurring in our child's life, whether it's health, finances, job, friends, education, marriage, etc. When an adult child or even an older teen becomes a prodigal, your passive parenting role escalates, whether you want it to or not. But "concern" can quickly intensify into "worry." The more you feel your hands are tied, the more energy you will invest in passive parenting. Passive parenting does not have to be ineffectual parenting, however. You can make it productive by channeling this energy into prayer (see chapter 11 for more on this topic).

Active parenting is a role that is constant at the onset of parenting and diminishes as a child grows older. Or at least it should. Some parents want to hang onto this role forever. They smother. They control, or attempt to. They see passive parenting as the first step to isolation and loneliness. Some parents may have made a healthy transition to passive parenting, but when the child becomes a prodigal, they want to shift back to the active role. With a younger child, a backward shift may be appropriate. But with a child eighteen or older, it has a negative effect. Ask yourself this question: If your adult child or older teen came to you and said, "I want to make my own choices, my own decisions, even if they are wrong," how would you respond?

"Why be so blind and stubborn? Listen to the wisdom of others." *That's control.*

"Why not talk to so-and-so before you decide. After all, what's the rush?" *That's control.*

"That's your decision. You know my values. You need to decide for yourself." *That's a loving relationship—and it's the approach with the best chance for success.*

Passive parenting goes counter to what you would like to do. Sometimes, we all want to reach out, shake our child by the shoulders, and say, "Shape up!" It's difficult to hold your tongue! But there is really no other option. You have to allow her to grow up, to learn from her mistakes.

Of course, there are limits to this policy. If you know he's going to deal drugs, shoot someone, take his life, or do something illegal, you wouldn't respond in this way. You'd have to take action. But if he wants to live a different lifestyle, join a cult, drink, smoke . . . there's not much you can do.

When the Prodigal Son asked his father for his inheritance, did the father believe he would use it frugally and wisely? Not likely. He knew. He knew that what he had worked so hard for over the years would be squandered in no time. It must have broken his heart to hand it over. But he did. He said, essentially, "It's your choice." He didn't try to control and he left the door open for a future relationship.

William Coleman tells the story of two families:

One night while watching television I saw two parents discussing their son's life in prison. He had committed a serious crime and was serving a term of eight to ten years.

I couldn't imagine the myriad of feelings they had to sort out, but I was intrigued by the decision they had made. Every couple of weeks they traveled to the penitentiary to visit their son. Those visits told me several things about these loving parents.

First, they were demonstrating to their son and to everyone else that this young man was still their son, no matter how sad the circumstances.

Second, they were willing to undergo an incredibly difficult task each time they made the visit. What did they talk about as they faced their son in the prison's impersonal visiting area? Were they able to laugh together? Could parents and child share experiences from their two different worlds? It must have been heartbreaking. Yet they were still willing to carry a heavy load for their son's sake, as well as for their own.

Third, they stuck to this commitment because they felt their son would not survive emotionally if they did not visit him. It was obvious that these parents loved their son and were concerned for his present and future welfare.

Their love was not dependent on his behavior.

It was not dependent on his situation.

It was not dependent on his future potential.

They loved their son where he was, as he was, and they wanted to express that love. Their devotion reminded me of the passage in Romans 14:3 where we are told, "for God has accepted him." Our heavenly Father is the model all accepting parents should follow.

In Kansas City two good, middle-class parents worked hard to hold their own in the midstream of life. They gave their son every consideration and a comfortable lifestyle. After high school he drove off toward the West Coast to carve out his own path.

Somewhere along the Pacific coastline he fell under the influence of cult members and soon joined their commune. He changed his clothes style, let his hair grow, and memorized the incantations.

When his parents discovered what he had done, they were badly rattled. This was a far cry from what they had envisioned for their oldest boy!

After recovering from the shock, his parents decided to travel to the coast and maintain their relationship. Although years have passed and their son remains in the cult, the parents have stayed in contact with this child who has gone off the deep end. Their love will not let them abandon their son. If he chooses to leave the cult, they want him to know that their love has never waned.[10]

How do you react to these stories? Can you see yourself responding in this way? The parents weren't agreeing with the choices their children had made. I'm sure they wished they could have yanked back the reins and changed the situations. But they knew they couldn't. They didn't try to control. They waited, loved, and accepted.

Instinct Versus Wisdom

Sometimes I've heard parents cry out, "I just don't know what to do!" We've all been there. And we all need the same thing—wisdom.

By wisdom the Lord laid the earth's foundations, by understanding he set the heavens in place. (Prov. 3:19).

I've heard parents say, "We need to trust our intuition." It's better to trust the wisdom of God.

The proverbs of Solomon son of David, king of Israel: for attaining wisdom and discipline; for understanding words of insight; for acquiring a disciplined and prudent life, doing what is right and just. (Prov. 1:1-3)

Look at these comparisons:

Instinct says: Stay alert. Don't let the problem escape your attention for a moment.

Wisdom says: Rest in God. Let Him give the situation His constant care and attention.

Instinct says: Stay in control or everything will go wrong.

Wisdom says: I will give God control and trust Him to take care of my child.

Instinct says: It's up to me to make things right, because I probably made them wrong to begin with.

Wisdom says: It's up to the Lord to make things right. I will hide in the shadow of His wings. I will relinquish my child and his problems to God.

Instinct says: I must win my child's approval.

Wisdom says: My child's approval is desirable, but not essential. God's approval is vital for me.

Instinct says: He's my baby. I just have to do it for him.

Wisdom says: He's an adult, or close to it. I love him, but he's on his own—and responsible to God now.

Instinct says: You must not rest!

Wisdom invites: Enter into the rest of God.[9]

We want our children to make wise decisions, but we as parents must also make wise decisions with regard to the way we respond to them. How can we be sure our decisions are good ones? James 1:5 gives us the answer.

"If any of you lacks wisdom, he should ask God, who gives generously to all without finding fault, and it will be given to him."

Throughout this resource, the book *Relief for Hurting Parents* by Buddy Scott has been mentioned repeatedly. Support groups based upon this book and the ministry of Buddy Scott are in existence throughout the country. If you are interested in starting or attending a support group, call 409-297-5700. If you are interested in ordering materials call 800-288-6333 or visit the Website www.buddyscott.com.

....

1. William and Candace Backus, *What Did I Do Wrong?* (Minneapolis: Bethany House Publishers, 1990), pp. 156, 157.
2. Rich Buhler, *Pain and Pretending* (Nashville: Thomas Nelson, 1988), p. 35.
3. Karen O'Connor, *Restoring Your Relationship with Your Adult Child* (Nashville: Thomas Nelson, 1993), p. 97.
4. O'Connor, pp. 55, 72, 73, 90, 110, 111, adapted.
5. O'Connor, p. 71.
6. Buddy Scott, *Relief for Hurting Parents* (Lake Jackson, Texas: Allon Publishing, 1994), p. 56.
7. Sidney Callahan, *Parents Forever* (New York: Crossroad, 1992), p. 48.
8. Callahan, pp. 51-52, adapted.
9. Scott, p. 56.
10. William Coleman, *How to Go Home Without Feeling Like a Child* (Dallas: Word Publishing, 1991), p. 13.
11. Backus, pp. 138-9.

CHAPTER EIGHT

Have You Released Your Child?

oted author Larry Crabb writes: When Kep was born, I gave him to the Lord and vowed to do my part in steering him in good directions, to fill his mind with the truth of God. I prayed the same prayer two and a half years later when Ken arrived. No parent worked harder to do it right: prayers every night; stories with a Christian point before they went to sleep; Saturdays given over to swim meets; afternoons to basketball games and karate lessons; annual father-son birthday meals (at the restaurant of his choice) when I asked each boy the same twelve questions, recorded his answers, and discussed them at the next year's birthday meal as a way of exploring development; a special thirteenth birthday trip with each son to introduce him to adolescence, complete with illustrated lectures on the birds and bees; return trips to the same fun spot on their twenty-first birthdays to launch them into adulthood.

When our boys were six and eight, I bought an overhead projector for family devotions. (How many dads have done *that?*)

Old Testament survey, New Testament survey, basic theology, book studies—we did it all. Discipline was consistent, including spankings followed by hugs and prayers. *What went wrong? What didn't I do?*

There was no lack of fun times. I once built a stand for Ken to sell a hot dog and lemonade lunch for fifty cents. He made twenty-one dollars. I spent thirty-seven.

When Kep showed the first signs of clear rebellion, I recall screaming at God: "What else do you want me to do? I've done everything I know!"

I also screamed at my wife. We were driving out of the parking lot of the Warsaw Health Food Store on Center Street when Rachael said, "Kep has his SAT exam tomorrow. What do you think he's doing right now in the parking lot outside the basketball game?" I pounded my fist on the dashboard of our car and yelled, "Why can't you let up on him?" She later told me that she felt blamed for all the trouble. Her words: "You made me feel that it was all my fault because I gave birth to him."

I hurt my wife. Badly. That kind of pain doesn't easily disappear. What words could I say, what deeds could I do that would have the power to soothe that pain, to touch the deepest part of her soul with healing love? How does a husband connect with a wife he has damaged?

During Kep's most difficult years, from fourteen to twenty, I grounded him, prayed for him, prayed with him, took long walks with him, bought him a car that I later sold as punishment. I remember using the well-worn line of frustrated parents: "I will not tolerate this kind of behavior while you are living under my roof." When he was eighteen, I told him that unless he committed himself to living by my standards (which I represented as God's), I would give him one hundred dollars and require him to leave our home.

I told him I loved him, I listened to him when he wanted to talk, I made firm decisions after taking his perspective into account, trying to give latitude wherever I could. I did everything I knew to do. Nothing reached him.

I know of nothing more agonizing than watching someone you love moving in a bad direction and feeling absolutely powerless to do anything about it.

What else could I have done? *What else could I have done?*

When he began his third year at Taylor, I purchased a small home on the outskirts of the campus for Kep to move into with several of his friends. Rachael and I helped clean the dirty floors and cabinets, cut the weeds so they resembled a lawn, and shopped garage sales for sofas, beds, and desks.

I had such a good dreams. My son would get involved in spiritual leadership on campus, the home would be a gathering spot for Bible studies, Kep would meet a wonderful Christian girl, take her to Ivanhoe's for ice cream after bonfire rallies before big games, and graduate with a bright future and a beautiful fiancée.

Maybe I was dreaming the wrong dreams.

But they seemed so right. I knew exactly what my son should become. I had no thought of *releasing* him. I wanted only to *control* him, to reduce him to someone predictable. I had my dreams. I'll never forget the time he turned to me during his last year of high school and said, with fury in every word, "You couldn't bear the thought of your son not going to college."

It was in that off-campus college home that Kep got into real trouble. And now he was expelled.[1]

Parental Beliefs

Beliefs are an important part of life. They give us direction, meaning, stability, and hope, among other things. Parents have beliefs about their roles as parents, about what they think is best for their children, and how they want their children to turn out. Some beliefs are good. They're healthy. Others are unrealistic and unhealthy.

Consider some of the following parental beliefs:

Some parents believe they own or possess their children. They see a child as something to be molded and formed in their hand. Too often, what they have tried to instill in their child is that the parents' needs, feelings, beliefs, and standards are what matters in life. It's as though the parents are looking for replicas or clones of themselves. If the parents are successful in this, they've helped their child develop into an emotional cripple, unable to separate his own identity from his parents'.

A child is not a possession to keep, but a loan of a life. Ties that bind like those described above have caused children to rebel in dramatic ways, severing themselves from any contact with home just in order to survive.

Some parents believe their adult children are accountable to them. It's difficult to let loose of the reins of accountability after all the years of guiding, consoling, supporting, and raising them according to the way we thought they should be raised. Do you ever struggle with the desire to tell your adult child "just one more thing" or to say, "If you'd just do this, you'd see what I'm talking about"? Maybe you think, "If only she'd listen and pay attention and do this!" She won't. Let her come to you. Once you've said something, remember, you've said it and it doesn't need to be said again. Once a child is grown, she must make her own decisions—and her own mistakes.

Some parents believe their children owe them (the parents) loyalty and thanks for all they've done. As one writer said:

> You clothed and fed them, gave them music and swimming lessons. You took them on vacations, sat up nights with them, rushed them to the hospital, and listened to their jokes. You helped with homework, volunteered in their classrooms, and threw parties and picnics to honor them. And what did you get for all your love and labor? "Not much," said one mother. "I haven't seen my son and his wife for six months and they live only thirty minutes away."
>
> Another mother said she's still waiting for her daughter to talk about the good memories of her childhood. "She has no problems remembering all the things I did wrong," said Vera. "You'd think she'd have a little gratitude."[2]

There's nothing wrong in hoping for appreciation. And they may give it, although perhaps not in the way or quantity that you hope for. Even if they don't, you can handle it. Sure, it's disappointing. It hurts. But remember the joy you received in giving those things. Let that be your satisfaction. Otherwise, you're letting what your child *isn't* doing determine your joy and happiness.

Some parents believe they will always have a close family. How will you handle it if your adult child doesn't live up to your expectations? Whether or not a child is a prodigal, he probably won't call or visit as much as you'd like. There may be occasions when he may withdraw for awhile. With a prodigal, it could be for a long while. The longer the silence, the more we parents tend to worry. We have this strong need to know everything that is happening. But we may not get to.

Some parents believe their offspring will always live by the parents' value system. Children will—and need to—sort out their own beliefs and values.

They need to be doing this all through their growing-up years in order to make their beliefs and values their own. If not, they will be vulnerable to many other influences. Unfortunately, the beliefs and values many prodigals develop are 180 degrees from our own and could also be in opposition to those of society. Hopefully and prayerfully, our children will discover their way. But it will have to be in their time frame.[3]

Hanging On

• It's difficult to let go of our children. It's a loss—there is no better word to describe it. Even if they are leaving for good things—going off to college, getting married—they are still leaving, and it hurts! And besides the pain of loss, relinquishing our children carries with it so many other implications. It could mean the end of your identity as a parent. Their leaving opens a hole in your life, and unless it's filled by new roles, it will become a constant companion.

What if your child is a prodigal? You may hear something besides "good-bye"—"I don't want or need the values that you tried to teach me." That hurts even more.

• It could mean you have little or no control over your child anymore (did we ever have as much as we thought we did?).

What if your child is a prodigal? Your efforts at rescuing or changing him hit a brick wall. They don't work. You feel inept, futile, impotent. The feelings of failure wash over you anew like a strong storm blowing in from the ocean.

• It could mean that you and your spouse don't have any glue to hold you together anymore—or, if you're a single parent, your emptiness and loneliness from a lost marriage could hit you all over again.

What if your child is a prodigal? The door is wide open now to blame one another for what the child is doing and what the other parent did or didn't do. When parents have a disabled child, or lose a child in death, the divorce rate is higher than with other couples. In this case as well, the situation can draw couples closer or drive them further apart.

• It could mean you feel disappointed over how the children turned out. Perhaps they aren't going to the college of your choice, or even to college at all. Maybe they don't attend church enough, haven't picked a worthwhile profession, don't work hard enough, etc.

What if your child is a prodigal? It's more than disappointment. It's hurt, a sense of futility, betrayal, outrage—and those feelings don't just pass away in time.

• It could mean that you can't protect your children from problems any longer, and you have to run the risk of their ultimate loss.

What if your child is a prodigal? With some prodigals, you may not even have contact, let alone the opportunity to protect. Some of the consequences of their actions may be extreme and they change the direction of your life forever. You wish the justice system you believe in for our society wouldn't apply to your child. You'd like an exception to be made by the system, by life, and by God.

• And finally, releasing your child means you're getting older—and we all know the implications of that!

What if your child is a prodigal? You may feel your age even more. If you're in your fifties or sixties, you have all the midlife issues to deal with for your own life on top of those associated with your child (and this could include caring for aging parents).

We all make mistakes as parents. Why shouldn't we? We're all amateurs in parenting. Most put in more time preparing to take their driver's license exam than they did to be parents. And the mistakes can run a wide range. The issue is not so much that they occurred, but more, are they continuing as the child moves through adolescence and into adulthood? The problem is that our mistaken ways may be all we know, and we've worked at refining them so well over the years that now we're not sure what else to do. This includes the roles we play in our families. We discussed these roles in chapter 5, but let's take another look again from the perspective of hanging on to grown children.

Revisiting the Roles
First, let's look at the *pleaser*. Putting others first and sacrificing for them

may not seem to be very harmful, but it is. It obligates others and generates guilt. It shelters your children from reality and retards their growth. Some parents continue to respond like this to gain their children's approval as well as their compliance. It's not a healthy way to live for either parent or child.

Next, let's look at the *rescuer*. Many children know just how to work their parents in order to be rescued. All they have to do is ask, and the parents cover the bills. It isn't the duty of the parents to be the bail bondsman for their children. We can't insulate or isolate our children. We don't need to experience guilt if a child needs help that we can't afford or choose not to give. In fact, by rescuing our children from their problems, it could be that we are interfering in what God wants to accomplish.

Another role is that of the *martyr*. Martyrs focus more on themselves than on what their children are experiencing. "After all I did . . .," "How could you do this to me?" and "They just rub my nose in all I gave to them. It's a terrible way to be treated!" are phrases martyrs use, often within earshot of the child. The purpose of these remarks is to control the child.

Parents who don't want to let go of their children are dependent on having them appreciate and acknowledge their relationship. They are afraid of severing the bond, of no longer being needed. Therefore, they fight the things their children do to gain independence.

Even if your adult child isn't living the way you would think he should, you need to stop fighting it. It may help to say the following to yourself, "He isn't responding the way I want. It's upsetting, but it's not the end of the world. I can handle this. I will survive. If he chooses to live this way, it's his choice and I can give him permission in my heart and mind to make his own choices. I will leave him in the Lord's hands and pray that God will bring others into his life that he will listen to."[4]

You see, there is a better way than control. It's called *relinquishment* and *detachment*.

Relinquishing Our Kids

The word *relinquishment* means to surrender a right, to put something aside, or to loosen one's hold on someone or something.

Isn't relinquishment abandonment? No. Relinquishment is *giving someone up,* whereas abandonment is *giving up on someone.*

- When you relinquish your child, you stop taking responsibility *for* him, but you still fulfill your responsibilities *to* him.

- When you relinquish your child, you're relying more upon God and less on what your child does or doesn't do.
- When you relinquish your child, you're freed from your emotional roller-coaster ride, since your feelings are no longer dependent on your child's response.
- When you relinquish your child, you give him the freedom to respond to God rather than to your pushing.
- When you relinquish your child, you're freed from your compulsion to bring your prodigal "back to the Lord."
- When you relinquish your child, you're able to see that you are not responsible for her choices—thus, guilt begins to diminish.[5]

When should you relinquish your prodigal?

You may have others admonishing you to "let go" of your child prodigal. God is the only one who knows when you are actually capable of doing this. Though you may be continually releasing your child to the Lord in your prayers, a specific time will come when God will ask you to let go, and he will then provide the strength to do it.

On May 15, 1976, Barbara Johnson drove to her church for a mid-week prayer meeting. It had been almost a year since her son Larry had disowned the family and disappeared into a homosexual lifestyle. She had been depressed most of the past year. This day was no different.

As she drove through the suburbs of Orange County, she felt the familiar burden inside. "I was tired of churning over Larry—tired of giving to God, and then carrying the heaviness myself. Over and over I thought I had taken my hands off and surrendered him to the Lord," says Barbara. "But I had been picking up my burden again and bringing it back home to carry around." She said out loud in the car, "God, I have had enough of this! Whether he kills himself, or if I never see him again, or if you take Larry's life, as you might do, or whatever happens—he is yours. I can't go on one more day with this overwhelming concern for him that's been consuming me for eleven months."

Knowing God had heard her decision, Barbara went into church and enjoyed the singing. Then as the pastor called for prayer for various situations, he said, "There is a mother here with a broken heart." Barbara had previously heard him say those words, and each time she knew the message was directed at her. She had even gone forward and asked for healing prayer. But today something was radically different. She sensed that the pastor was not talking about her any longer. She wanted to get up and shout, "Pastor, it's not me! It's not me!" For the first time in almost a year, his reference to a brokenhearted mother was someone else.

"I practically flew home," Barbara remembers. "My heart sang. The music just flowed out of me. The only explanation for my lightness in spirit was that I had allowed God to keep the burden of Larry. When I had finally stopped asking God, 'Why me, Lord?' and turned it around to 'Whatever, Lord,' then the burden actually lifted and I was free in my own spirit to expect God to work."[6, 7]

Detaching from Our Kids

Another mother was struggling with an adult son who was a drug user as well as a convicted felon. She had taken him into her home and he had robbed her. She had paid for his hospital stay and intervened on his behalf with the authorities. Nothing had worked. People had been encouraging her to "detach," but she didn't understand what this meant. This is what she said:

It took me a long time to know what they were saying. They kept telling me, "Detach. Detach. You must detach yourself from Russell."

I thought they meant detach myself, walk away from him completely . . . and I argued. I would sit at those meetings and argue with that. I said, "Do you mean to say that if I was on a beach and saw someone on a bridge about to jump, that I wouldn't get out of my comfortable beach chair, and go over and try to help them? I couldn't do that."

But what they meant was, "Don't detach yourself from *Russ*, but from *his problems*." And I have done that, I have finally been able to do that for the first time in my life. It's just happened in the last few months, not even a full year. But I've reached a point where I know, intellectually, emotionally, whatever, I know that I have done as much for Russ as I can do. I can do no more. There is nothing more that I can do, financially, physically, mentally.

I can continue to love him, which I will do; support him; be by his side at all times. But he must assume the responsibility for his actions now and know that if he takes a drink or pill, *he* is going to pay the consequences.

I hurt for him. I just cry, and I'd die for him. I can do no more for him.[8]

Detachment happens when parents recognize that their child is a separate being—and that the responsibility for another person has recognizable limits. Detachment is necessary for the parents' emotional survival, as well as for the child's independence.

But detachment isn't easy, nor does it "just happen." It's a choice. Perhaps it's best illustrated like a bee sting. When a bee stings you, it flies off. It's out of your life. Now you have a choice. You can leave the stinger in, and the sting will fester and become infected. It will be painful, and you could become quite sick because of it. Or, you have another option. You could remove the stinger, and the sting will hurt for only a short time. One day the pain won't be there at all. You'll remember that you were stung by a bee and that it hurt. But healing will have taken place. *It's a choice to stop suffering so much.* Time *does* help this process.[9]

This is how one mother detached from a sexually promiscuous runaway daughter:

I was devastated. I gave myself and my daughter time and space to work through things. I was desperate. I told God that I didn't have the strength to forgive and love her, but that I was willing for Him to do those things in me. I can't explain how it happened, but He did it as I kept pursuing His love through me to her. I feel compassion and love for her now and am able to reach through all the stuff to her and see her as a valuable person. I stopped using Scripture with her and feeling that I had to do or say something. I pray often, asking God to set a guard over my mouth. I was releasing her to God and I had peace. Years ago I put her name on a slip of paper with the date and put it high in my cupboard. When I would come across it, I'd release her again and add a new date. Some of us need tools and this was one that helped me figuratively release her. I had to reach way up high in the cupboard to deposit the slip.

She has two sons. I love them dearly and help when I can

with them. She likes that. I try to bless her with encouragement
and take an interest in her life.

The following poem expresses the meaning of letting go beautifully.

Letting Go
To let goes doesn't mean to stop caring,
it means I can't do it for someone else.

To let go is not to cut myself off,
it's the realization that I can't control another.

To let go is not to enable,
but to allow learning from natural consequences.

To let go is to admit powerlessness,
which means the outcome is not in my hands.

To let go is not to try to change or blame another,
I can only change myself.

To let go is not to care for,
but to care about.

To let go is not to fix,
but to be supportive.

To let go is not to judge,
but to allow another to be a human being.

To let go is not to be in the middle arranging all the outcomes,
but to allow others to effect their own outcomes.

To let go is not to be protective,
it is to permit another to face reality.

To let go is not to deny,
but to accept.

To let go is not to nag, scold, or argue,
but to search out my own shortcomings and to correct them.

To let go is not to adjust everything to my desires,
but to take each day as it comes.

To let go is not to criticize and regulate anyone,
but to try to become what dream I can be.

To let go is not to regret the past,
but to grow and live for the future.

To let go is to fear less and love more!

—Author Unknown

Do you need to let go of your prodigal child? In what ways do you need to relinquish and detach?

....

1. Larry Crabb, *Connecting* (Nashville: Word Publishing, 1977), pp. 2-3.
2. Karen O'Connor, *Restoring Your Relationship with Your Adult Child* (Nashville: Thomas Nelson, 1993), pp. 212-213.
3. O'Connor, pp. 208-215, adapted.
4. Dorothy Eaton Watts, *When Your Child Turns from God* (Hagerstown, Md.: Review & Herald, 1996), pp. 26-29, adapted.
5. Anita Worthen and Bob Davies, *Someone I Love Is Gay* (Downers Grove, Ill.: InterVarsity Press, 1996), pp. 73-75, adapted.
6. Worthen and Davies, p. 73.
7. Barbara Johnson, *Where Does a Mother Go to Resign?* (Minneapolis: Bethany House, 1979, 1994), pp. 116-117.
8. Jo Brans, *Mother, I Have Something to Tell You* (Garden City, N.Y.: Doubleday & Co., 1987) p. 76-77.
9. Brans, pp. 194-195, adapted.

CHAPTER NINE

Preventing
and Intervening

I'm a mother of four children. My second oldest is thirteen and going on twenty-three one day and three the next. Sound like a roller coaster? It is! Everything seems to be a battle and she's determined to win. But so am I. So our home is a battleground. Some days our weapons are ballistic. I've had all sorts of questions about her. 'Is she ADD, ADHD, strong-willed, oppositional, just plain stubborn, or normal?' I don't want a war and I don't want her to end up rebelling and going off the deep end. What can I do *now* that might prevent her from becoming like her older brother? We don't need any more drugs, theft, or involvement with the law!"

These kinds of questions are raised time and time again by parents who either have a prodigal and see the signs developing in another child, or who want to do some preventive work well in advance of their child becoming a prodigal.

What kind of children rebel?

I've seen strong-willed children rebel.

I've seen compliant children rebel.

I've seen well-balanced, independent children rebel.

I've seen first-born, second-born, third-born, and last-born children rebel.

I've seen children rebel whose parents anticipated rebellion. I've seen children who don't appear to have a rebellious bone end up rebelling.

There are no guarantees with regard to which children will rebel and which children won't. *Every* child has a rebellious bent because of his sin nature. That's a given. Some rebellion occurs just in the heart and mind; some is translated into action. Some ends quickly; some never ends.

Having said that, however, there is one temperament type that is perhaps more likely to rebel than the others. Dr. William Carter, in his book *Child Think*, describes it like this:

> An *oppositional child* is one who seems to be in constant conflict with adults and the word *cooperation* is not in his vocabulary. And he tends to be consistent in his behavior.

Characteristics of the Oppositional Child

Let's take a look at the characteristics of an oppositional child:

- *The oppositional child enjoys being in control, so he challenges authority* figures. He is driven to win, so his relationships with adults are characterized by power struggles. He sees adults as standing in the way.
- *The oppositional child has a tendency to remain negative, even though the negativism serves no purpose.* He seems to hold on to his right to be negative or upset forever, even after everyone else has settled down. It doesn't seem to make sense, but for this child, his emotional reaction serves the purpose of demonstrating his ability to be stubborn. Your efforts to get your child to calm down are seen as invading his right to do what he wants. For most children, when their emotions rise, they express them, and the feelings diminish. But this child hangs on to his feelings, refuses to allow them to be taken away from him—even when it is to his advantage.
- *The oppositional child would rather compete than cooperate.* It's almost as though he's an adrenaline addict. He craves and loves the excitement, the conflict, that competition generates. He enjoys frustrating others and enjoys the power of controlling

others. Even negative attention is acceptable since it generates conflicts. This child is afraid of losing, so he provokes Mom and Dad to keep problems alive. He doesn't know where the line of competitiveness ends and aggression begins. The results he receives from his interactions just serve to feed his competitive drive. Cooperation and working together don't appeal, since others slow him down or block what he wants.

- *To an oppositional child, right and wrong are somewhat relative.* Right and wrong, in this child's mind, generally seem to be determined by the consequences of his behavior. For this child, if he's caught doing something wrong, then *perhaps* he will think that what he did was wrong. If no one saw him, he probably will think that it wasn't wrong. Thinking this way frees the child from experiencing guilt. If this approach is really deeply ingrained within the child, I would suspect inadequate conscience development. However, this is certainly not the case with all oppositional children.
- *The oppositional child is frustrating, since he doesn't respond to normal discipline techniques or approaches.* What you try may not work, since the value you place on what you do or offer probably doesn't have the same value for your child.

If you try to use a reward system he may care less.

A strong punishment is "no big deal."

This child may see more value in intimidation, fighting, having a "bad" reputation, or making others ill at ease than he does in rewards or punishments.

To this child, real punishment is more likely to be your refusing to argue, to debate, to get upset, or even to stay around talking to him. When you withdraw, he loses control—you don't.

- *The oppositional child is not dumb.* Early on, he discovers that others don't understand him, and he enjoys this. If he's punished, but he got his parents upset, it's worth the punishment to him.

Why is a child like this? Is there one cause, or a multitude of them?

Children are born with many different temperaments. Unfortunately, this is one of them. Often, you can identify this child as a toddler. It's just part of his natural makeup. But remember, oppositional behavior can be reinforced and strengthened by the parents. Dr. Carter says:

> The oppositional child tends to want to take charge of all his own decisions sooner than he is able to responsibly do so. When parents place barriers before him to prevent the harm that would inevitably arise from the child's lack of judgment, the child looks for other ways to satisfy the desire to be in control. In most cases, parents end up reinforcing this child's behavior.[1]

Even an argument leaves this child with the feeling he has won. Why? Rather than relying on Mom and Dad to give him a sense of security, this type of child relies upon control for security. He'd rather do everything for himself. He tries to wrestle control away from his parents. He wants to make his own decisions far sooner then he's capable of doing so. And how do we reinforce and reward him? By letting him draw us into a power struggle and get us emotionally upset. He's actually able to take charge of the emotions of his parents. *When he feels emotionally in charge of an adult, he's being rewarded.* It's as simple as that! But we as parents have (or should have) more control over our emotions than a child, even an irritating child.

If we parents engage in a power struggle, it may encourage the continuation of oppositional behavior. Often, these struggles can become intense and ugly. It's easy for a parent to look for some punishment that will do the job—something strong enough to control the child and convince him to give it up and behave as he should. But the child realizes what the parent is doing and won't budge. So the parent intensifies his or her efforts to stay in control, as does the child, and the conflict continues. *Remember, when the child has taken charge of your emotions, he has won.* You can't resolve this problem by forcing a solution. If you override and dominate the child, he will go underground like a mole that's out of sight under the surface of your yard, but is still able to destroy it.

Dealing with the Oppositional Child

What's the best way for a parent to respond to this child, as well as aid in his character development?

The most important tip I can give you is to control the emotions—your own. These are your child's finest tools for controlling you. When your oppositional child opposes you, you need to disengage emotionally.

If you can detach yourself from her problem behaviors, you will get a much better response. You don't necessarily need to hide your emotions from your child, but you would be better off simply stating them in a matter-of-fact way. When you show anger, you've lost. Your child knows she's won when you blow up.

So what do you do with your anger? The angrier you are, the lower your voice should be. This shows that you're still in control. You'll have many feelings during a confrontation, but don't let them get the best of you. One thing you can say is this (being sure to use a calm voice): "This problem is really yours. If you would like to become upset over this, that's all right. However, you need to figure out a solution as to what to do. It's your choice, and you have the capability to work it out."

Stay out of arguments. You'll lose. Remember what the Word of God has to say:

A fool gives full vent to his anger, but a wise man keeps himself under control. (Prov. 29:11)

It is to a man's honor to avoid strife, but every fool is quick to quarrel. (Prov. 20:3)

When arguing with a rebel, don't use foolish arguments as he does, or you will become as foolish as he is! Prick his conceit with silly replies! (Prov. 26:4-5, TLB)

How can a parent stay calm enough to accomplish this? It's possible. I've seen it. You really don't want your child to be opposing you, do you? No. Have you been able to get her to stop what she's doing or the way she's responding to you? If not, quit fighting her head-on. Do the opposite. In your heart and mind, give her permission to be the way she is at this time in her life. Tell yourself you can handle it. Remind yourself that your child covers up her insecurities by responding in this way. By doing this, you will take pressure off yourself and be able to disengage emotionally and respond differently. For awhile, you may not be changing the child, but you can change yourself.

This is a child who needs boundaries. You cannot force them upon her, since she needs to come to her own conclusions about the wisdom of what she does. One of the best ways to respond is to give her choices that have consequences—and the consequences create boundaries. The child has to accept the consequences for what she does. Allowing children to experience the logical and natural consequences of their actions provides an honest and real learning situation. (This does not include situations that would be dangerous or injurious to the child).[2]

Above all, your oppositional child needs to have choices, when you're getting along and when you're not. She is driven inside to take control, and it is up to you to give her some positive ways in which to have control. Choices reduce the power struggle. Whenever you tell your child to do something you can't make her do, you give her too much control. When you offer choices, use phrases like:

"Would you rather . . . ?"
"What would work best for you?"
"Feel free to go ahead and do that, but it will have to be somewhere else. Or feel free to stay here without doing it. It's your choice. You decide."

Remember these guidelines:

- Be sure you offer choices you can live with, since your child will know the one you don't like and select it every time.
- Don't give any choice unless you're willing to allow him to experience the consequences of his choice.
- Don't give a choice unless you're willing to make the choice for her in case she doesn't or won't.[3]

Set up situations or give instructions in which the child is able to make a choice between two or three acceptable alternatives. This allows you to continue to control the overall situation while giving the child some control as well. It also lets the child know that he has some voice and choice in the matter. As well, it teaches him that he must accept the consequences of his choice. "John, you will have to make a decision. You can go to Jim's house this evening to work on your car and fix the garage door tomorrow night, or you can fix the door tonight and go to the game with Jim tomorrow night. You make the choice and I'll go along with it." Or "Mary, you need to wear a dress to this event. You can wear the brown dress or the green dress. You choose."

A child also can be given a choice as to when he does his homework. As long as he chooses to earn good grades, he may choose when to do his homework. If he chooses to earn poor grades, however, then he has made the choice to do his homework immediately after school. Either way, the decision is his—as are the consequences.

When I was a youth pastor, I didn't have one oppositional teen in my group—I had several! We would have some youth meetings of 100 to 150 kids. I learned an approach then that worked well. I simply told them that it was a privilege for them to be able to be in this meeting. If they chose to listen and pay attention, they were choosing to stay. If they chose to talk and be disruptive, they would be making the choice of being asked to leave. That was all I said. I waited for the first one to be disruptive and then escorted him out. The others knew the rule would be enforced if they made that choice. It worked. When using an approach like this, be sure you use the phrase "you have a choice."

Another way of staying out of a power struggle is to tell your child what *you* are going to do, not what *he* is going to do.

Let your child know what you will allow, what you are willing to do, and what you will provide. For example, let's say your child is upset, angry, and snickering at you. Can you think of what you usually say or are tempted to say? Probably something along the lines of "Don't you dare say that to me. You just settle down or you won't be getting any privileges around here!" And your anger intensity probably goes out of sight as well.

That response invites conflict and anger, as you well know. Telling her instead what *you're* going to do may confuse her and throw her off her preset plan, and that's good!

Just think for a moment. Can you really enforce statements like:

"Don't use that tone of voice!"

"Don't use those words!"

"Don't look at me like that!"

"Don't curl your lip up in a sneer!"

Imagine what might happen if you were to say instead, "I'd be glad to hear what you have to say when your voice is as quiet as mine and when your anger isn't so intense. Take some time and think about it. I'll be glad to talk with you about it later."

You *don't* have to:

Raise your voice

Make threats

Say, "Do it or else!"

And remember:

You *give up power* when you talk about the other person.

You *gain power* when you talk about you.

Drinking and Driving

Alcohol and driving is a common problem with teenagers, whether they are oppositional or not. It seems pretty straightforward to tell your adolescent, "As long as you live here you will not drink. There's no debating this. I don't ever want to smell liquor on you when you come in from being out. And I mean it. You do it once and you'll see what happens." However, that's an invitation to be tested. A better way to put it is this: "If I don't have to worry about your drinking, then I won't have to worry about your using the car when it's available. How's that sound to you?"[4]

The authors of *Parenting Teens with Love and Logic* give an excellent example of how one parent handled this situation:

Phil's seventeen-year-old daughter, Tiffany, comes home with alcohol on her breath. Should Phil talk to her about it immediately or in the morning? *Morning*. With anger or sadness? *Sadness*.

"Oh, I felt so sorry for you last night," Phil says the following morning. "I smelled alcohol on your breath. I'm starting to worry about you and alcohol. What would you guess about using the family car now?"

"I guess I might not get to use it," Tiffany replies.

"Good thinking," Phil replies.

Did Phil set a limit? Yes. Is Tiffany going to try to talk him out of it? Absolutely. Can she? No. Because no matter what Tiffany says, Phil can say, "Probably so."

"But I won't do it again," Tiffany begs.

"Probably so."

"Well, all the other kids get to do it."

"Probably so."

"Well," says Tiffany, trying to draw her father into an argument, "so you've got a big problem over alcohol, Dad, and now I can't drive and I've got to look like a dork at school because—"

"Probably so."

"Well," she persists, "how am I supposed to get to work at the jewelry shop?"

Now Tiffany's trying to give her problem to her dad. If Phil gives her an answer, will she like it? No. It would be better for Phil to say, "I don't know. I was going to ask you the same thing."

"Well, I'll get fired!"

"Probably so."

Phil knows that if he gets angry with Tiffany, he will strip the consequences of her drinking of their power. By expressing anger he will insert himself into the process and impede the logic of the consequences from taking effect. By using "probably so" and keeping the focus on the effects of drinking and driving, Phil prevented Tiffany from focusing her anger on him. Instead, she was continually forced into facing the lesson taught by the consequences of her drinking.[5]

Connie was an adolescent who ran away to Canada one summer with a girlfriend. She had felt smothered by her parents, and she stayed away until the following winter. Notice how her parents responded when she wanted to come home.

When Connie phoned home, her mom and dad showed no anger. Rebellious teens love anger, but there wasn't any to react to.

"Well hi, honey!" they low-keyed it. "Where have you been?"

"Vancouver," answered Connie.

"Well, that's a nice city. You been having fun up there?"

"Oh, yeah."

"What have you been doing?" they inquired politely.

"Waiting tables and bumming around," Connie filled in.

"That's good! When do you think you're coming home?"

"Now?" asked Connie.

Then Mom said, "Well, that would be wonderful! We'd be glad to see you again! Let us know when you're coming in, and we'll be there."

"How will I get home?" Connie pressed.

"Well, honey, how did you get there?"

"I thumbed it," Connie replied, waiting for her mother to gasp in horror and rush in to rescue her from doing it again.

(Connie's mom knew Connie was going to say that, because we had already rehearsed this conversation in my office. You know what rebellious teens are going to say long before they say it. They're often not very creative).

"Well, Connie, how do you plan to get home?" her mom said.

"I don't know," came a little tremulous voice.

"Is there something we can do?"

"I'd like you to help."

"Hmm, Connie," Mom answered. "I've always felt that if you got yourself somewhere you should get yourself back. However, I would be willing to send you half the fare for a bus trip home if you found out how much it would cost and how we could mail the money to the bus company. Of course, you'd have to pay us back with interest after you returned home and got a job here."

A moment of silence. Then Connie said, "Okay—I'll find a job, and then I'll come home on the bus."

"Hey, good thinking!" Connie's dad chimed in. "It probably beats thumbing home in the winter. It's cold! And of course, it's better than taking the risks of getting beat up or raped."

"Debbie's already gone because her parents paid airfare for her return," Connie said, with some resentment.

"I know, dear," Mom said. "That probably was convenient. But this is what we are willing to do, and we'd love to see you. You got yourself there by thumbing. The bus trip probably should be better than that, right?"

Acquiescing, "I guess you're right."

See how these parents are handling it? No anger, no punishment, just pure questions and consequences.[6]

How the Bible Describes a Prodigal

Once you have a prodigal, there are a host of questions you want answers to. "Is there a chance that my child will straighten out his life? "How can I know whether I can trust her again?" "If I bring him back into the house—or let him remain—will that hurt the other children?"

The Book of Proverbs has some guidelines for us that can help. It begins by giving us a word to describe our wayward son or daughter—it's the word *fool*. There are actually three Hebrew words that are translated into this one English word. One of them means a kind of "thickness" that manifests itself in "moral perversions" rather than in mental stupidity. The person is foolish, not because of any lack of mental capabilities, but because of refusing to submit to any directives other than his own.

The second word reflects the idea of "lacking foresight." It's the tendency to make wrong choices because of having never adequately matured. Regardless of his age, this person still acts like an adolescent, making impulsive and immature decisions.

The last word conveys the idea of being "empty-headed," or lacking moral sensitivity. He doesn't have the sense of right and wrong that most people have.

What are the characteristics of a fool?

- First, a fool hates learning. In fact, he has no openness to the fact that he even *needs* to learn.

How long . . . will . . . fools hate knowledge? (Prov. 1:22, NASB)

- Next, a fool is defensive. When he is corrected, he puts up a wall. He rejects what is said. He won't learn from anyone about anything. We're all defensive at some time, but the fool is that way all the time.

> Understanding is a fountain of life to him who has it,
> but the discipline of fools is folly. (16:22, NASB)

- Also, a fool thinks he knows it all. And when you know everything, why be open to learning?

> A fool thinks he needs no advice, but a wise man listens to others. (12:15, TLB)

> A fool rejects his father's discipline,
> But he who regards reproof is prudent. (15:5, NASB)

> A wise son makes a father glad,
> But a foolish man despises his mother. (15:20, NASB)

- A fool has a hard time learning because his mind is going in all directions. His attention is scattered. He may have ambitions, but he doesn't carry them out because he gets distracted.

> Wisdom is in the presence of the one who has understanding,
> But the eyes of a fool are on the ends of the earth. (17:24, NASB)

- One of the other characteristics of a fool is his inability to control his tongue. One author said, "His mouth is a minefield and every time he opens it he puts his foot on a mine."[7] How graphic!

A fool always loses his temper,
But a wise man holds it back. (29:11, NASB)

A fool is quick-tempered;
a wise man stays cool when insulted. (12:16, TLB)

• A fool has little or no self-control. He's impulsive. His lack of
control with his own life is one of the things that causes the fool
to be such a pain. Also, he opens his mouth and lets it rip without regard for anyone else. In this way, he adds to the burdens
of others. What he shares affects them. When he explodes, the
shrapnel hits those around him.

A stone is heavy and the sand weighty,
But the provocation of a fool is heavier than both of them. (27:3,
NASB)

• A fool soon gains the reputation of being hot-headed. And
when his temper flares up, stay away.

Keeping away from strife is an honor for a man,
But any fool will quarrel [burst out]. (20:3, NASB)

Make no friendship with a man given to anger,
and with a wrathful man do not associate,
lest you learn his ways and get yourself into a snare. (22:24-25,
AMP)

• A fool is also known by his senseless comments. He's a person
whose mouth is in constant motion without much to say.
There's no depth.

Even a fool is thought to be wise when he is silent. (17:28, TLB)

His mouth is his undoing!
His words endanger him. (18:7, TLB)

• A fool is negative about others to the extent of being slanderous.

He who conceals hatred has lying lips,
and he who spreads slander is a fool. (10:18, NASB)

The wise man is glad to be instructed,
but a self-sufficient fool falls flat on his face.
(10:8, TLB).

• A fool is prideful. One of his favorite topics of conversation is himself. His pride seems to swell out of his mouth. He's full of himself.

In the mouth of the foolish is a rod of pride. (14:3, KJV)

• A fool's mouth gets him in trouble. The more he says, the worse it gets. He could take a lesson from a wise man.

A wise man holds his tongue.
Only a fool blurts out everything he knows;
that only leads to sorrow and
trouble. (10:14, TLB)

• One of the sad things about a fool is his inability to handle success.

Like snow in summer and like rain in harvest, so honor is not fitting for a fool. (26:1, NASB)

Snow doesn't belong in summer, nor does rain during harvest time. They're out of order, out of sync for the season. They don't fit. Frost in the summer kills the crops. Honors given to a fool don't fit and in the long run destroy him. He's unable to handle them.

• A fool shows no ability to handle money. He squanders it rapidly.

Luxury is not fitting for a fool: much less for a slave to rule over princes. (19:10, NASB)

Of course, it's not only prodigals who have these characteristics. You may even see one or two of them in yourself! But if you saw a description of your child in that list from Proverbs, you'd be wise to take Proverbs' advice on how to deal with him.

How to Handle a Prodigal

If you want to work out problems in a relationship with a fool, Proverbs says, "Don't expect much."

> When a wise man has a controversy with a foolish man, the foolish man either rages or laughs, and there is no rest. (29:9)

You end up dealing with unreasonable and objectional responses. They're also usually way out of proportion to the issues. The fool either justifies himself with defensive anger or laughs at the issue. Not only that, but he ridicules the concept of forgiveness.

> Fools mock at making amends for sin, but good will is found among the upright. (14:9)

The word *amends* means "a guilt offering." A fool looks at the available forgiveness and, not only is he not thankful, but he holds it in contempt. A fool sees this concept as a sign of weakness. It gets worse.

> "Doing wickedness is like sport to a fool; and so is wisdom to a man of understanding" (10:23, NASB).

His attitude toward breaking the law and the legal system is oppositional. A fool has a deficit when it comes to moral reasoning. He laughs at the system. The only thing wrong to him would be to stop doing wrong things.

> Desire realized is sweet to the soul, but it is an abomination to fools to depart from evil. (13:19, NASB)

What's the best way to respond to a fool? Answer a fool carefully.

> Do not answer a fool according to his folly,
> lest you also be like him.
> Answer a fool as his folly deserves,
> lest he be wise in his own eyes. (26:4-5, NASB)

You don't want to lower yourself to his level, but there are times where you must give him a direct answer. If not, he may perceive your silence as approval. Another guideline is to be careful giving him responsibility. It's best not to.

He cuts off his own feet, and drinks violence
who sends a message by the hand of a fool. (26:6, NASB)

Like a thorn which falls into the hand of a drunkard,
so is a proverb in the mouth of fools.
Like an archer who wounds everyone,
so is he who hires a fool or hires those who pass by.
(26:9-10, NASB)

If you put a fool in such a position, you could end up paying for the consequences. You'll end up hurting yourself by giving such a person responsibility.

Can a fool really learn? Decide for yourself.

In the mouth of a fool a proverb becomes as useless as a paralyzed leg.

A proverb is an educational tool. But not to a fool. If you spend time trying to educate him, you could be spinning your wheels.

You also should avoid giving honor to a fool. "Like one who binds a stone in a sling, so is he who gives honor to a fool" (Prov. 26:8, NASB). It doesn't fit the fool and it's useless. He'll damage the honor.

This next principle is a difficult one, especially for a parent. Because a fool can influence others into approaching life as he does, the writer of Proverbs suggests we're better off not spending much time with him—or allowing our other children to.

He who walks with wise men will be wise,
but the companion of fools will suffer harm. (13:20, NASB)

Can the fool change? *You* can't change him. *He* can't change himself. The fool has to be willing to open his life to the teaching of Scripture and allow God to work within him to bring about the change. *Only* the work of the Holy Spirit can change a person.

Paul said, "For to us God revealed them through the Spirit; for the Spirit searches all things, even the depths of God. For who among men knows the thoughts of a man except the spirit of the man, which is in him? Even so the thoughts of God no one knows except the Spirit of

God" (1 Cor. 2:10-11, NASB).[8]

So, back to the questions raised at the beginning of this section . . . As you look at what Proverbs says, does this pattern fit your child? You might say, "For the past two years, it has." And if so, that's just recent, not a lifelong pattern. It's as though she's playing the part of a fool, rather than it being a long-standing, deeply ingrained pattern of living. There's more hope for her than one who has lived like a fool for many years. However, if your prodigal's behavior does reflect these characteristics, be very cautions about having this person in your house, whether or not you have other children. Her presence could be detrimental to those who live there. And if you see a younger child leaning this way, it may help to seek counseling for her immediately.

It isn't easy to hear your son or daughter described as a fool. But the writer of Proverbs knew how you feel, and he addressed that as well.

A rebellious son is a grief to his father
and a bitter blow to his mother. (Prov. 17:25, TLB)

Take comfort in knowing that your feelings are understood . . . and in fact, they are understood by One who has parented many a prodigal. He'l be with you every step of the way.

1. Dr. W. Lee Carter, *Child Think* (Dallas: Word Publishers, 1991), pp. 11, 12.
2. Carter, pp. 1-31, adapted.
3. Foster Cline and Jim Fay, *Parenting Teens with Love and Logic* (Colorado Springs: Piñon Press, 1992), pp. 65-66, adapted.
4. Cline and Fay, pp. 69, 70, adapted.
5. Cline and Fay, pp. 71-72.
6. Cline and Fay, pp. 228-229.
7. Kenneth T. Aiken, *Proverbs* (Philadelphia: Westminster, 1986), p. 102.
8. Robert Hicks, *In Search of Wisdom* (Colorado Springs: NavPress, 1995), pp. 171-200, adapted.

CHAPTER TEN

When Your Child
Divorces

T here's an event occurring more and more frequently in family life today, one that can shatter not just one family, but several. The results seem to linger, not just for years, but forever. Whether your adult child or (in the case of your in-laws) someone else's is the prodigal in this situation, it can change your life as well as theirs.

It's when an adult child divorces.

The shock of discovering that this is happening can be especially upsetting and unsettling for the parents of the divorcing child.

Just as when your children married you could feel that imaginary string stretch, so when they divorce you can feel it shrivel. The family expands and contracts with every addition or subtraction of a member. When divorce strikes your family, through your child, the alliances and divisions throughout the entire extended family shift, even break.

When divorce occurs and you experience so many pushes and pulls on near and dear relationships, it is useful to think of your family as a mobile. If you cut the string between any two parts, it unbalances the whole structure, until it is repaired. Your whole family reverberates when your child divorces and the mobile goes on tilt.[1]

The parents' marriage can sometimes be affected by the different ways the wife and the husband handle pain and grief. They may have different ideas about how to respond to their son or daughter, to their ex-daughter- or son-in-law, and to their ex-in-laws.

Upset Value Systems

Parents may feel that their child's divorce threatens their entire value system. If they are totally opposed to divorce, regardless of the reason, they will certainly face a difficult time because their sense of values has been violated. They may struggle with how to explain it to others. They may experience guilt if they feel they failed to hand along their value system to their child.

Parents may discover that the breakup of the marriage is due to their child's unfaithfulness. Some parents have found it necessary to deal with diseases such as AIDS in the fallout. And what if the marriage failed because their own child abused his spouse?

Parents in such situations should be prepared for an onslaught of anger once the shock of their child's situation hits them. They may find themselves brooding over the divorce for many weeks or months. While they are doing the dishes or driving alone, they may fuss and stew about how easily their child and partner gave up on their marriage. Lives are disrupted by the breakup, and they may have anger at what caused it, who caused it, and how all this is affecting everyone involved.

Unanswerable questions arise. "Why didn't they work it out or go for help? Why didn't they see this coming? Why are they giving up so easily? Where's the effort that every marriage takes?" Although parents want to be supportive, a part of them disagrees strongly with what is going on. They begin to worry and wonder how this will affect their child's job and self-esteem, as well as their financial future.

Parents begin to anticipate all the losses and changes they themselves will experience because of this divorce. Family vacations, family visits, birthdays, and holiday gatherings will change. They won't be viewing the video of their child's wedding so often, if at all. And what about the extended vacation they were planning? Does the divorce change all this?

The anger may be accompanied by a need to blame, and they will have a number of targets upon which to vent. This could include the in-laws and the attorney. Frequently, the parents of a divorcing child begin blaming their spouse for what he or she did or didn't do that contributed to the problem. They may find it helpful to write some unmailed letters to those with whom they are angry, to help them release those feelings.

Parents may take some of the guilt and blame on themselves. They begin to take stock of what they did or didn't do, to doubt their adequacy as parents and as in-laws. If they have largely stayed out of the couple's life, they may feel they should have been more available. Perhaps more advice would have helped. Perhaps they should have helped them more with the rent or volunteered to baby-sit more so they could go out as a couple. They wonder if they couldn't have helped out more financially, spiritually, and emotionally. Or perhaps they feel they helped too much, to the point of interfering in their lives.

What about the Grandchildren?

Much pain will center around the struggle and pain of the grandchildren as they try to work through their parents' breakup.

If the adult child is the noncustodial parent, grandparents will end up losing and hurting more, because they will probably find it more difficult to spend time with grandchildren. They are in the most powerless position. Even if custody is retained, their concern won't end. They may find it all too easy to fall into the trap of doing too much for the grandchildren as a way of compensating for their pain and sadness.

In a study of freshmen at two major universities, 96 percent said their grandparents were "extremely important" or "important" in their lives. And 90 percent said they wish they could have spent more time with their grandparents than they did.

It may be helpful to know that all states have visitation laws for grandparents, and grandparents will be able to visit their grandchildren as long as they are able to show that it is in the best interest of the children.

But what exactly is in the best interest of the children? How can the grandparents best help them?

The grandchildren will need plenty of love and acceptance. They need to have confidence in something that gives them stability. Grandparents will be their connection with the past. At first it may feel like walking on eggshells to be around them. The grandparents may be at a loss to know what to say, and they don't know what the grandchildren might ask. The best a grandparent can do is to be available, and to listen. They should let the grandchildren initiate the discussion, and they can check with their adult child to see what the children have been told and what the parents would like to have said.

As grandparents move into this new and awkward role, they will need to deal both with their own concerns and with those of the grandchildren. Will there be enough money to care for them properly? Will they become latchkey children, coming home to an empty house? What if the custodial parent has his or her new romantic interest stay overnight, or, worse, move in? How will this divorce affect the grandchildren's sense of self-esteem and their academic performance? How will their birthdays, Little League games, and trips be handled?

Grandchildren may raise their own concerns and questions, either directly or through their behavior. If you are that grandparent, here are some common concerns of grandchildren and some responses you can give:

1. *"Who will take care of me?"* Reassure them that you can, at intervals or for a period of time. Adolescents need a kind of baby-sitting too.

2. *"Is there anything in the world reliable and predictable?"* Grandparents should make special efforts to be there for them as promised, every time, barring emergencies. When you say you're going to pick them up or meet them, get there on time. Your reliability is crucial.

3. *"Are my parents crazy?"* When the opportune moment arises, you can explain what an unsettling period this is for both parents and that after awhile, they and the children will settle down more and more.

4. *"Where is my father/mother now living?"* Encourage visits to the absent parent's home if that meets with the custody arrangements. The grandchildren want to feel part of the new setting.

5. *"Will my mother/father—my custodial parent—get sick, hit by a car, or worse?"* You can't promise this won't happen, but let your grandchildren know that you are a backup and so are the cousins, uncles, and aunts from both sides of the family.

6. *"Will we have enough money now?"* Reassure them they will be taken care of. You can help with money or gifts to your grandchildren, giving a

weekly allowance or money for a class trip.

7. *"Will I have to change schools now?"* Tell them that many children remain where they are and attend the same school. But if change is in the wind, research the positives in the new school and visit the classroom if you can.

8. *"Will I have to move to a new neighborhood?"* Recount the stories of the times you moved, of your new room, new friends, and the yard for a dog. If the move is nearby, reassure them that their old friends can visit and stay overnight.

9. *"Is Mom going to marry Bob? Will they keep me with them?"* You probably can't do much about this one except to wonder with them.[2]

What about the "Ex-Laws"?

Perhaps one of the most awkward dilemmas is how to relate to your ex-in-laws. Terri, the mother of a newly divorced son, told me, "Fred wanted me to cut off all contact with his wife's relatives, as he had done. But I told him, 'Fred, you may have divorced your wife, but I am not divorcing her mother, Ethyl. We've developed a wonderful friendship and prayer partnership over the past fifteen years and we have both stated that it will continue. You will just have to learn to accept it.'"

You may always be closer to your child's first set of in-laws than the next set. If you relate better to them and that is your choice, nothing is wrong with that. Or perhaps you never did relate well to the in-laws, and this isn't a major loss for you. You may end up resenting the other grandparents. Some grandparents have also had to go to court to ensure their own visitation rights. But if your child had children in the marriage, you may always have some contact and interaction with the other set of grandparents.

If you were especially close to your son-in-law (or daughter-in-law), alienation will add to your pain. Although he may have destroyed the marriage, you may find it difficult to dislike him if he was the son (or daughter) you never had. You feel a push-pull tension and cry out, "Why did this have to happen?"

Refilling the Empty Nest

If your child is a needy or dependent person, you may have more of a struggle because your heart goes out to her—and you may end up doing more for her.

It is not uncommon for a divorcing adult child to move back home for financial reasons. This requires adjustments on the part of all concerned. Jay Kesler writes of this situation first from the viewpoint of the adult child:

> When divorced adult children live in the house belonging to their parents, they naturally feel impotent, unable to cope. They feel as if they're not adult; they have failed. As parents of divorced children, we can repeat, "This is working out all right; it isn't a problem; you're not in the way." But still, grown children who are forced to take charity from their own parents feel demeaned and will often react in bizarre and unpredictable ways. Their loss of self-esteem may cause them to engage in withdrawal, in acts of self-denigration, or sometimes even in hostility. They may lash out in anger against the situation, not realizing that they have picked the wrong target. We always hurt the ones we love because they are close to us.[3]

Of course, the grandparents have major adjustments to make too. Perhaps the new arrangement will affect the proposed sale of your home, which used to be too large. It may also change retirement plans. Jay Kesler continues:

> Grandparents can be caught in the middle trying to do the right thing, to be loving and charitable. We often may need to spend a good deal of time in prayer, coming to terms with understanding our divorced children, forgiving them their outbursts and irresponsible behavior. We must realize that there is a much larger principle at stake here and attempt to provide an environment in which our grandchildren can grow into normalcy and somehow escape the ravages that divorce breeds.[4]

Money Matters

Unfortunately, another major element can complicate things, and it may also prolong the period of adjustment to a divorce. It's called money.

Your child may need or want to borrow from you to pay the rent during a separation.

You may be approaching retirement and find yourself pulled between saving for yourself and helping your daughter with the bills after she is awarded custody of the three children.

You may be upset over your child's irresponsible financial behavior and decide to assist your daughter-in-law or son-in-law and the grandchildren rather than your own child.

You may be struggling about having given the ex some family heirlooms, never dreaming that there would be a divorce and that she would keep the heirlooms.

Maybe you gave the couple the down payment on their house as a wedding gift, but now the house is the ex's.

These and other financial issues may pertain to past gifts and loans. But you can do little about those. You can, however, plan for the future. Parents of a divorced child ask questions such as these:

> How can I be sure my child's ex doesn't receive any of my child's inheritance?
> How can I be sure the ex doesn't misuse funds I've set aside for the grandchildren?
> How can I get out of business arrangements with the ex and his or her family?

Just as your child needs assistance from an attorney, you may find yourself in the same situation.

New Branches on the Family Tree

In time, a semblance of stability may be reached, only to be upset again when you learn that your family tree is about to have some unfamiliar branches grafted onto it. For instance, your child has just told you that he/she is getting married again . . . to someone with three children. You are going to be an instant stepgrandparent. It is out of your control, and you have no choice in the matter.

Sometimes, however, you can't help but resist. Several common problems can occur—all of which need to be avoided.

- *The new spouse is not welcomed in her new in-laws' home, or, at best, is politely tolerated.* I have seen situations in which the new marriage was not even recognized. In one case, the new wife was referred to as "that woman and her children." This is classic, unhealthy denial! In some cases, the new marriage is sabotaged by the grandparents through rejection, manipulation, or the spreading of rumors.

- *Sometimes the new spouse is accepted, but the stepgrandparents can't bring themselves to become involved with the new stepgrandchildren.* This is less of a problem if the children are adolescents or older than if they are younger.
- *One of the most common problems is unequal and unfair treatment of grandchildren and stepgrandchildren.* This is a difficult situation because the grandparents' feelings for their original grandchildren are usually positive, and it is natural for them to feel that the others have been thrust upon them.

This is an issue that needs to be discussed with your child and his or her new spouse, clarifying expectations and intentions. You will have to work out some creative solutions and will find no perfect answer. Younger children have difficulty understanding preferential treatment. Older ones can learn to understand that grandparents will do more for their own grandchildren, whom they have known from birth, than for others. They can accept this as long as the differences don't blatantly emphasize feelings of being discounted and rejected.

You may want to talk with the new in-laws, asking how they would like you to relate to their children and sharing your own concerns and struggles. Many who have taken this step have found some workable solutions. One stepgrandmother was surprised and relieved to discover her new daughter-in-law didn't expect her to take her children to the lake each summer as she did her own grandchildren and didn't want her to feel obligated to do so.

- *Yet another problem can arise when a grandchild is born to this new marriage.* The grandparents may tend to favor the new child because it is part of their family line, and this will be obvious to the stepgrandchildren.

In any case, feelings cannot be forced to develop. However, you may be surprised to find blessings in the new relationships as time goes on. The new children may never have had the opportunity to have grandparents, and you could end up filling some unmet needs. You may discover a kinship with the new grandchildren or even the new spouse you never expected. But neither side should force themselves upon the other. Give it time. Learn how to pray specifically for the newcomers. In some cases, the new members of the family may not have been involved in church, or they may not be Christians, and they can become your mission field.

Drugs and Other Dependencies

Today we are facing a new generation, one that has a different set of values and morals than the ones we were raised with. Parents are shocked and frustrated over their adolescent child's choice of dress, friends, lifestyle, sexual preference, attitudes, education (or lack of), and vocation, and this can happen when the child is in his teens, twenties, thirties, or even forties or older. Following are three specific areas in which such frustrations are often experienced.

Substance Abuse

I have seen the use of alcohol and drugs cause a marriage to self-destruct. One mother told me, "It's such a shock. Jim never drank or used drugs as a teen nor through college. And now to discover he's been using up his and his wife's income to support his cocaine habit is just too much. And to think we lent him several thousand dollars last year to get his business going! It all went for drug use."

When parents have invested years and tears in an adult child, only to see him destroy his life with drug abuse, it is natural for them to not only be shocked but try to help. The difficulty is that parents are sometimes the last people an adult child will listen to.

At the other extreme, some adult children expect criticism—perhaps even preaching—from their parents, and in some strange way actually depend on this reproach to justify their habit. This can easily lead to a "codependent" relationship, with you as a parent providing the very impetus for your son's dependency.

The goal of parents whose child's lifestyle they reject should be to make their own value system clear and to show loving concern without being lured into the codependency trap. They will need to practice detachment. This does not mean aloofness or disdain or rejection. It means that they free themselves from compulsions to correct their child's behavior for him. It means that they communicate by their actions that they have their own lives to live, and that their adult child is responsible for his life. This is the detachment that has been referred to throughout this book.

Sometimes detachment even motivates and frees people around us to begin to solve their problems. We stop worrying about them, and they pick up the slack and finally start worrying about themselves. What a grand plan! We each mind our own business.[5]

Extramarital Relationships

It can be heartrending for the parents to learn that their own child has been unfaithful to his spouse, or that he has otherwise sought sexual relationships beyond the boundaries clearly set in the Scriptures.

How do you handle it if you are told by your child that he's homosexual, and his involvement with "friends" has destroyed the marriage? What explanation do you give your three grandchildren when they ask why their parents are breaking up? And how would you deal with your concerns about the possibility of AIDS and other sexually transmitted diseases?

In such situations, parents of adult children often ask themselves several questions: "What was our contribution to this problem? Where did we go wrong? Why didn't we see any indications of homosexuality when they were young? Did we just close our eyes to them? How do we explain the reason for the breakup to our friends?" Some basic considerations can bring stability in an otherwise uncertain time when such events occur.

Parents often have trouble distinguishing the personality boundaries between themselves and an adult child when the child rejects the values he was taught. They may feel that something in their parenting was an unwitting invitation to their child to somehow become involved in a lifestyle that was foreign to what the parents openly espoused.

It may be helpful to remember that one way adult children become adult is through the process of *individuation*—consciously and unconsciously separating themselves from their parents.

Although parents may agonize over their adult child's lifestyle choices, they can only affirm this process of becoming an individual. They don't need to second-guess their parenting styles or their own values and ideas regarding sexuality. Instead, they can reaffirm that they and their adult child are separate persons, able to make differing choices regardless of having come from the same family—even if you strongly disagree with his choice.

Your child's extramarital lifestyle will require you to find a balance between accepting him as a person, while making it clear you reject his actions. Usually, the parent-child relationship is so close that you won't need to make long or frequent speeches to communicate your disappointment. You may want to be honest about any anger. But the same process of individuating that led him to adopt a different set of values means he will likely resist any sermonizing or tongue-lashing you may feel like delivering.

Parents in this situation can certainly reaffirm their own value system by means such as making it clear that their child's illicit partner won't spend the night on any visits to their home. When others bring up the subject, they can certainly affirm their own feelings and values. It is never an easy situation, but a course must be sought that allows you to affirm your child as having been made in the image of God, while standing firmly for God's will for His creatures.

Parents of adult children do not need to tell others more than they wish. Honesty can prevail even while being discreet, and it is fine to describe their child's situation in general rather than specific terms. Although saying something such as, "They just reached a point where their marriage couldn't work," may not satisfy some people, true friends will respect your right to privacy and that of your child.

Such discreteness can be balanced by confiding with a pastor, counselor, or an especially close friend, and sharing the truth in order not to lapse into denial or unwisely block your feelings.

But remember that your child may work through this problem and return to a biblical lifestyle. If he does, you will regret having broadcast the news of his problem, especially if you did it out of anger and retaliation.

Rejected Faith

Sylvia Vogel, a Jewish mother, faced a different kind of disappointment in her relationship with her adult daughter Ellen:

> From the beginning, the mother was aware of the implications of her daughter's actions. Yet she was unable to stop them. On Mother's Day, (she) received word that the Moonies had picked her Jewish daughter and a black seminary student she hardly knew as one of 705 "perfect matches" for marriages.[6]

Even if the break from the parents' faith is not as drastic as this, any deviation from so precious a heritage as a family's traditional belief in God can be traumatic. Again, some parents suffer from guilt when this happens. Doesn't the Bible say that if you bring up your child in the way he should go, when he is old he won't depart from it (see Prov. 22:6; for further illumination, read chapter 3 of this book)? The fact is, you may not have been perfect in training your child in a religious faith. But accepting imperfection, as we have previously noted, is often the first step toward healing a wound. One father shared with his pastor his feelings of guilt over a grown daughter who had rejected his faith: "I was busy having a midlife crisis about the time my daughter was a teenager and struggling with her faith."

Life does become complicated when our grown children make choices we'd rather they didn't. But our own faith and the presence of Jesus will see us through the times of personal and family storms.

....

1. Dorothy Weiss Gottlieb, Inez Bellow Gottlieb, and Marjorie A. Slavin, *What to Do When Your Son or Daughter Divorces* (New York: Bantam Books, 1988), p. 37.
2. Gottlieb, Gottlieb, and Slavin, pp. 119-120.
3. Jay Kesler, *Grandparenting: The Agony and the Ecstasy* (Ann Arbor, Mich.: Servant Publications, 1993), p. 16.
4. Kesler, p. 16.
5. Melody Beattie, *Codependent No More* (San Francisco: HarperSan Francisco, 1987), p. 57.
6. Joy P. Gage, *When Parents Cry* (Denver: Accent Books, 1980), pp. 16-17.

CHAPTER ELEVEN

Praying Parents

I prayed for this child, and the Lord has granted me what I asked of Him. So now I give him to the Lord. For his whole life he will be given over to the Lord." And he worshipped the Lord there. (1 Samuel 1:27-28)

How are you praying for your child? What *is* the best way for parents to pray for their child while she's living the prodigal lifestyle? Is there a set way, a formula, principles or guidelines to follow?

Even before you consider how and what to pray for, remember that the first step is doing what Hannah did in the passage quoted. She gave her child back to God. She relinquished her child.

Years ago a Christian publishing house came out with a ministry to help prospective parents. It was called the Cradle Roll Program. This program provided written materials to assist parents who were preparing for the birth of their child. The material was called *Loan of a Life*, which reflected the fact that children don't really belong to us. *They're not our possessions.* We've been entrusted with their care for a few short years, but in the natural progression of life, they will be relinquished to form their own families. At that time, we have to turn them and their lifestyle over to the Lord. That's not so difficult if they are making choices that we approve of. But if they are not . . . it's excruciating.

What is the kind of praying that is needed during this time of crisis? One of the best descriptions of a parent praying comes from Stormie Omartian in her book *The Power of a Praying Parent:*

> Prayer is much more than just giving a list of desires to God, as if He were the great Sugar Daddy/Santa Claus in the sky. Prayer is acknowledging and experiencing the presence of God and inviting His presence into our lives and circumstances. It's seeking the *presence* of God and releasing the *power* of God which gives us the means to overcome any problem.
>
> The Bible says, "Whatever you bind on earth will be bound in heaven, and whatever you loose on earth will be loosed in heaven" (Matthew 18:18). God gives us authority on earth. When we take that authority, God releases power to us from heaven. Because it's *God's* power and *not* ours, we become the vessel through which His power flows. When we pray, we bring that power to bear upon everything we are praying about, and we allow the power of God to work through our powerlessness. When we pray, we are humbling ourselves before God and saying, "I need Your presence and Your power, Lord. I can't do this without You." When we don't pray, it's like saying we have no need of anything outside of ourselves.
>
> Praying in the name of Jesus is a major key to God's power. Jesus said, "Most assuredly, I say to you, whatever you ask the Father in My name He will give you" (John 16:23). Praying in the name of Jesus gives us authority over the enemy and proves we have faith in God to do what His Word promises. God knows our thoughts and our needs, but He responds to our prayers. That's because He always gives us a choice about everything, including whether we will trust Him and obey by praying in Jesus' name.
>
> Praying not only affects *us,* it also reaches out and touches those for whom we pray. When we pray for our children, we are asking God to make His presence a part of their lives and work powerfully in their behalf. That doesn't mean there will always be an *immediate* response. Sometimes it can take days, weeks, months, or even years. But our prayers are never lost or meaningless. If we are praying, something is happening, whether we see it or not. The Bible says, "The effective, fervent prayer of a right-

eous man avails much" (James 5:16). All that needs to happen in our lives and the lives of our children cannot happen without the presence and power of God. Prayer invites and ignites both.[1]

Now, does this mean that you receive everything that you pray for? No. Of the 650 prayers in the Bible (not including the Book of Psalms), only 450 of them have recorded answers. **All prayers are answered, but according to the wisdom of God.** Jesus did say prayers would be answered—"Everyone who asks receives" (Matt. 7:8)—but the answers could be yes or no, direct or indirect, immediate or deferred. One thing we can be certain of, though, is that our prayers are responded to by a loving God.

> Which of you, if his son asks for bread, will give him a stone? Or if he asks for a fish will you give him a snake? If you, then, though you are evil, know how to give good gifts to your children, how much more will your Father in heaven give good gifts to those who ask him! (Matt. 7:9-11)

If you want to see an example of a parent who prayed for his children, look at Job. In the first chapter of the Book of Job you discover that, after Job's children feasted, Job had them purified. "Early in the morning he would sacrifice a burnt offering for each of them, thinking, 'Perhaps my children have sinned and cursed God in their hearts'" (v. 5). He was concerned and faithful in bringing them before the Lord.

John Bunyan made an interesting comment about prayer many years ago. He said,

> You can do more than pray
> after you have prayed
> But you cannot do more than pray
> until you have prayed.

Another author said:

> When a mother prays for her wayward son,
> no words can make clear the vivid reality of her supplications . . .
> She does not really think that she is persuading God
> to be good to her son,

for the courage of her prayer is due to her certain faith
that God also must wish that boy to be recovered from his sin.
She rather is taking on her heart the same
burden that God has on his;
is joining her demand with the divine desire.
In this system of personal life which makes up the moral universe,
she is taking her place alongside God
in an urgent, creative outpouring of sacrificial love.
Her intercession is the utterance of her life;
it is love on its knees.

—Harry Emerson Fosdick

And the Bible even suggests a prayer we might use:

God . . . grant them repentance leading them to a knowledge of truth
. . . that they will come to their senses and escape from the trap of the
devil, who has take them captive to do his will. (2 Tim. 2:25-26)

One of the guiding passages of Scripture for the way we're to pray is found in 1 Thessalonians 5:17(KJV): "*Pray without ceasing.*"

What does that mean? It means frequent, brief prayers expressed while we're walking, waiting on hold, driving (with eyes open!), or at any time. God is not concerned about the setting, but only that we pray. You want to saturate this child in prayer.

As parents, we need to pray constantly for our children. What can we pray for? Well, everything, but if you want specifics, here are a few:

Pray for your children to be protected from physical, mental, and emotional harm.

Pray for their spiritual growth, character development, and help with any character defects.

Pray for their views and attitudes about themselves.

Pray for their ability to say no to temptation.

Pray that they will turn away from wrong directions they may be going.

Pray for their daily difficulties.

Pray for the friendships they are choosing.

Pray for them to remember that you love them.

But above all, praise God for these children, for who they are and who they can become.

Cheri Fuller described what one mother did when her college-age son was arrested for selling drugs:

> She read her Bible passage until she felt the Holy Spirit stopping her at a verse.
>
> Then she wrote that verse on two 3 x 5 cards—one went in a clear frame on the kitchen sink and the other on her car's dashboard—and asked God to teach her something about His character revealed in the verse. She would praise Him for that attribute all day. *God, not the problem, was her focus.*
>
> As she got quiet before God and allowed Him to speak to her, she also looked for some truth about herself, her husband, and her children in the verse. Throughout the day she concentrated on that verse for each person, especially Trent. "I'd envision what it was going to be like when that verse was true about him. I'd thank God that it was going to happen in His timing, which brought me a tremendous peace," she says. By conscious discipline, she shifted her focus from his rebellious attitude to who he is as a child of God. The storms at home didn't dissipate right away, but over time her attitude changed, and she grew excited about what God was going to do.
>
> One verse she chose was Ephesians 2:10, which says, "For we are God's workmanship, created in Christ Jesus to do good works, which God prepared in advance for us to do." This verse reminded her that her children were God's workmanship—not hers. God's craftsmanship is impeccable, and He finishes what He starts. He had already prepared them for "good works," and she prayed they would respond to His leading.[2]

When her son was arrested and sentenced to several months in jail, he described the next events in a letter he wrote from jail to the thirty people who had been praying for him:

> After I got arrested with multiple felony drug charges, I had no idea how drastically and quickly God would do His work. Before my arrest, my life was selling drugs. I was indifferent to my family and wasting my education. God rescued me from the depths of my despair by raiding my apartment and instantly cleaning out the physical impurities of my life. From that point God took care

of me and began to work on my life. He let me out of jail, even though my bail was set at $50,000, brought me home to a spiritual family and friends, and gave me only six months in jail when I could have had years in prison.

Jail was the most awesome time of my life. I had the privilege to leave this world and my old life and hang out with God for four months. He turned me completely inside out as I learned and experienced the strength of His perspective. My life is now His, and I cannot wait to see what He does with it. I know that it was the prayers of many which kept God so close to me and held my eyes on Him so I could see no other way. Sometimes I wish I could measure the power of prayer because I'm sure it's the greatest power we have. And the best gift we can give to anyone else. Thank you so much for your prayers. May the love of God touch your life as it has touched mine.[3]

Sometimes parents become discouraged when they pray. Their children still have problems and they feel God isn't granting their requests. If you've been there, consider these words of wisdom from another parent who has struggled:

We parents must allow our concept of prayer to be shaped by scriptural reality, for then we will understand that our prayers are not tools with which to manage God. Rather, the opposite is the case, because God uses our prayers to manage us, to bend our will to him and brand our soul with his character.[4]

Almost all parents resist giving up on a child. But sometimes you feel as though you talk, you pray, you reason, you look for help wherever possible, and yet nothing happens. You're worn out. If you are on the verge of giving up, you're probably familiar with the phrase, "I'm ready to throw in the towel!" Maybe you just don't feel as though you have any more to give. As one man said, "There's nothing left for me to do. I feel empty. I don't have any hope left."

John Karetji, a pastor from Indonesia, says he made that statement during a difficult time in his life. A man came to him and asked if he knew where the phrase about throwing in the towel came from. He replied that he didn't. The man went on to tell him that it's a phrase used in boxing. When the manager standing outside the ring sees that his fighter can't make it any longer in the boxing match, he throws the towel into the ring, signifying that they are giving up.

Did you notice? It's not the boxer who has the towel, only the manager. Only the one who sent the boxer into the ring can throw in the towel.

We may feel like the boxer who wants to call it quits. But we were sent into the ring of life by someone else. *Remember who it was who sent you into the ring!* Jesus said, "I will never leave you nor forsake you" (Heb. 13:5, NKJV) and "Lo, I am with you always." (Matt. 28:20, NKJV)

In Matthew 7:7 (NASB) we read, "Ask, and it shall be given to you; seek, and you shall find; knock, and it shall be opened to you." We are to keep on asking, seeking, and knocking. Persistently!

Did you ever hear of a woman swimmer by the name of Florence Chadwick?

Nearly fifty years ago—in 1952—she attempted to swim the channel from Catalina Island to the California coast. She had been the first woman to swim the English Channel, so this effort wouldn't be a new experience for her. But the day she set out was a difficult one. The water was very cold and the fog was so thick she could hardly see the boats around her. To make matters worse, the water was infested with sharks, so her trainers in the boats around her used rifles to drive them away. On and on she swam for over fifteen hours, in spite of the intense chill of the water and the sharks. But finally she felt she couldn't go any farther, and she asked her trainers to bring her into the boat. They encouraged her to stick with it, since they were so close to land. But Florence couldn't see anything but fog, and she quit.

When she got into the boat, she saw that she was only a half-mile from shore. She had stopped in sight of her goal.

Sometimes we parents do this as well. It seems that nothing changes, and we get discouraged. But we're called to press on. Keep putting forth the effort. Keep praying.[5]

> "See, I will send you the prophet Elijah before that great and dreadful day of the Lord comes. He will turn the hearts of the fathers to their children, and the hearts of the children to their fathers; or else I will come and strike the land with a curse." (Mal. 4:5-6).

God can restore a wayward child to relationship with his family—if we're willing to love, forgive, and keep on praying. Our forgiveness, however, will never equal that which God offers us and our children, including the prodigals.

One parent described what she went through with their son and how she prayed. "Our prodigal made it clear he had rejected our value system when he told us he was homosexual," this pastor's wife said. Here is her story:

> When you finally learn the truth about your child—usually after having suspected it but not wanting to face it—you are emotionally shattered. The pain is beyond description. You feel you can't talk to anyone for fear other members of the family and colleagues in the ministry will learn the terrible truth.
>
> There were times when I struggled with intense anger toward Ed. I sometimes felt he was rebelling against everything we ever believed in as the ultimate means of hurting us and destroying his dad's ministry. At those times, I was tempted to blame my husband for not being a more attentive father. However, the Lord showed me who the true adversary was in Ed's life and in our family—it wasn't my son or my husband. My attitude changed.
>
> Later, when we could talk with him without getting angry, I began to empathize with the enormous pain of rejection he had suffered as a teenager. He dropped out of church because he felt he would never find acceptance there. He said the only place he could feel accepted was in the gay community.
>
> "This is the way I am, so you may as well get used to it," he told us. "I wish it were different, but I've felt this way for as long as I can remember. I've asked God to change me, and he hasn't. The unhappiest years of my life were when I tried to deny that I'm gay. Since accepting it, I've been happy. I have a relationship based on mutual respect, not just on sex."
>
> Obviously our son is deceived by the enemy to think he was born like this, because that view is totally contrary to Scripture. But it's useless to argue with him. We can only ask the Holy Spirit to reveal truth to him—which we've done for years. It has been a long, painful battle to pray for him without giving in to despair.
>
> We've learned to lean on God like never before. He has helped us to show love to our son and keep the lines of commu-

nication open. The Lord also has provided a few trustworthy prayer partners who are standing with us. Our confidence in His faithfulness is rock-solid, and we refuse to be moved by visible circumstances. While Ed knows that we do not condone his lifestyle, he knows, too, that we love him deeply and have forgiven him. Sometimes he even calls home to ask for prayer.

To other parents suffering this trauma with their children, I can offer this assurance: As they keep their confidence in God, and continue to pray and seek His help to walk in forgiveness, they will begin to see a light of hope at the end of a long, dark tunnel.

One of the newer approaches to praying for children is to "pray the Bible" for a child. This is simply using passages of Scripture to formulate prayers, or actually saying the verses back to God, making them your own petitions. This is definitely a biblical practice, since we see it modeled again and again in the Scriptures.

Jesus and His disciples sang the psalms together as part of morning and evening prayers. And when Jesus was experiencing His greatest agony on the cross, He cried out the words of a psalm: "My God, my God, why have you forsaken me?" (Ps. 22:1).

Many other Bible passages are recorded prayers. Some of the best known are the prayer of Moses after the escape through the Red Sea (Ex. 15); Hannah's prayer at the temple (1 Sam. 2); Jeremiah's lament over Jerusalem (Lamentations); Jonah's plea for grace (Jonah 2); the song of Mary after the angel's visit (Luke 1:46-55); The Lord's Prayer (Matt. 6:9-13); Jesus' prayer for His disciples (John 17:6-19); and Paul's prayers for a young church (Eph. 3:14-21).[6]

There is tremendous value in praying the Scriptures.

It's a way to help us resist becoming stuck in a rut. Perhaps you're different, but there are times when I experience a prayer blockage. Words, ideas, and phrases seem to have taken a vacation from my mind. It's difficult, not only to get started, but to keep it flowing. Scripture gives us structure as well as direction. And it's also a way to pray specifically for what your child needs at this time.

Too, it's a way to remember God's character, promises, past faithfulness, and goodness, which we tend to forget. It's a memory activator. It helps to bring balance into our own thought life. Jeremiah said, "Yet this I call to mind and therefore I have hope: Because of the Lord's great love we are not consumed for, His compassions never fail" (Lam. 3:21-22). When you pray the Scriptures, you can know that you are praying in God's will. Scripture can be used to evaluate our motives and reveal the direction for our prayers.

It also helps us pray with a greater sense of confidence and expectancy. When we focus on God's promises, we have a greater assurance of what He will do. We also learn to trust Him for accomplishing what He will do in His own way and time.

When we pray the Scriptures for our child, we grow in our own personal relationship with the Lord. We are reading the love letters that God has written to us. And reading these by praying them for our children instills His words within us even more.

Finally, praying in this manner opens us so that the Holy Spirit can minister to us.[7]

Quin Sherrer and Ruthanne Garlock have given us some helpful suggestions in this regard.

One especially effective tactic involves personalizing verses of Scripture as you pray, such as replacing the pronouns with the names of the children or people for whom you're interceding. For example, Psalm 23:3 could be personalized in this way: "Thank you, Lord, that you guide my son Keith in the paths of righteousness for your name's sake." The verse takes on added potency as both an expression of praise to the Lord and a declaration of truth to the enemy.

We pray differently for children during various phases of their lives. For instance, the following prayer for a child who is either a student or an employee combines several verses:

Lord, may my child like Daniel show ". . . aptitude for every kind of learning, [be] well informed, quick to understand and qualified to serve in the king's palace" (Dan. 1:4). May he/she "speak with wisdom and tact," and may he/she be "found to have a keen mind and knowledge and understanding and also the ability . . . to solve difficult problems" (Dan. 2:14; 5:12). Lord, endow my child with "wisdom and very great insight, and a breadth of

understanding as measureless as the sand on the seashore"
(1 Kings 4:29).

Another way to personalize these same Scripture verses would
be to speak them aloud about your child: "My child will be found
to have a keen mind and knowledge and understanding and ability to solve difficult problems. He/she does have wisdom and
insight and breadth of understanding as measureless as the sand
on the seashore." By hearing the Word of God—even from our
own lips—we stand firm on his truth as applied in our very own
family. And in doing this we have strengthened our own faith.[8]

Consider this passage as another example of one suited to the prodigal child:

I pray that out of his glorious riches he may strengthen you with
power through his Spirit in your inner being, so that Christ may
dwell in your hearts through faith. And I pray that you, being
rooted and established in love, may have power, together with all
the saints, to grasp how wide and long and high and deep is the
love of Christ (Eph. 3:16-18).

When you pray for your children, do you also pray for yourself?
What changes need to be made in your own life? Sometimes the
insight of other parents can help us develop sensitivity to these issues.
Consider the following parents' prayers.

Lord,
I submit myself to You. I realize that parenting a child in the way
You would have me to is beyond my human abilities. I know I
need You to help me. I want to partner with You and partake of
Your gifts of wisdom, discernment, revelation, and guidance. I
also need Your strength and patience, along with a generous
portion of Your love flowing through me. Teach me how to love
the way You love. Where I need to be healed, delivered, changed,
matured, or made whole, I invite You to do that in me. Help me
to walk in righteousness and integrity before You. Teach me Your
ways, enable me to obey Your commandments and do only what
is pleasing in Your sight. May the beauty of Your Spirit be so

evident in me that I will be a godly role model. Give me the communication, teaching, and nurturing skills that I must have. Make me the parent You want me to be and teach me how to pray and truly intercede for the life of this child. Lord, You said in Your Word, "Whatever things you ask in prayer, believing, you will receive" (Matt. 21:22). In Jesus' name I ask that You will increase my faith to believe for all the things You've put on my heart to pray for concerning this child.[9]

Dear God,
I am powerless
and my life is unmanageable
without Your love and guidance.
I come to You today
because I believe that
You can restore and renew me
to meet my needs tomorrow
and to help me meet the needs of my children.
Since I cannot manage my life or affairs,
I have decided to give them to You.
I put my life, my will,
my thoughts,
my desires and ambitions in Your hands.
I give you each of my children.
I know that You will work them out
in accordance with Your plan.
Such as I am,
take and use me in Your service.
Guide and direct my ways
and show me what to do for You.
I cannot control or change my children,
other family members or friends,
so I release them into Your care
for Your loving hands to do with as You will.
Just keep me loving and free from judging them.
If they need changing, God,
You'll have to do it; I can't.
Just make me willing and ready
to be of service to You,

to have my shortcomings removed,
and to do my best.
I am seeking to know You better,
to love You more.
I am seeking the knowledge of Your will for me
and the power to carry it out.

—Anonymous

David and Heather Kopp give us specific examples of how to pray for the character development of children.

Dear Lord,
I spend all day trying to shape my children's characters, but it only works from the outside. I'm afraid I may not be getting through. Lord, You hardly look at the outside because You know that the inside is what matters (1 Sam. 16:7). How can I teach my children integrity?

I worry sometimes that my kids will grow up having mastered all the right words and actions but not be changed through and through by You. Then they'll fold when the pressure mounts.

Lord, use Your Spirit and Your Word to penetrate their innermost natures (Heb. 4:12). Make them whole and healed all through so that the beauty people see on the outside is true of their hearts as well. Only You can accomplish this, Lord.

Save my children and me from deceiving ourselves—and along the way keep making us whole all through by Your work of grace (Ps. 119:29).
Amen

Lord Jesus,
It is my joy and honor to pray for my children. Each one is a miracle in the making, growing from year to year into a creation that only You can see completely (Ps. 139:16). I absolutely believe in this miracle going on right under my nose!

Yes, O God of miracles, I know it's happening—in spite of ill, cranky, foolish, wandering, and obstinate kids (and their parents). I know it's happening in spite of my inability to see the miracle or on some days even to care much about it. Yes, You are up to something grand here! Lord, today I ask that You would grow in my children the courage to want, reach for, and cherish Your best. We do not want to be like those who give up on our destiny and are lost (Heb. 10:39, PH). You changed cowardly, small-spirited fishermen into world ambassadors, leaders, and heroes of faith. Change us too, Lord! You are able to do immeasurably more than all we ask or imagine, because Your immense power is at work in us (Eph. 3:20).

Fearfulness and timidity are *never* what You give! Your gifts to us through Your Spirit are

- power to overcome all obstacles
- love that changes us and those we love
- self-discipline to stay the course (2 Tim. 1:7).[10]

You can pray for immediate specific concerns as well as for specific future issues.

Quin Sherrer and Ruthanne Garlock suggest a unique approach to praying for children—keeping a personal prayer journal. (I highly recommend their book *How to Pray for Your Children.*) This is what Quin says:

For nearly 25 years now I've kept personal prayer journals, which I fill with requests, words of praise, reports of answered prayers and specific lessons I'm learning through prayer or Bible reading.

In the first section of my notebook, I glue a picture of LeRoy and myself and write out our prayer Scriptures. The next three sections contain pictures and prayer requests for our three children and their families. The last section is reserved for others outside our family. Here I place names (and a few pictures) of young people I pray for in the mission field, my children's friends, relatives and some government officials.

In the section for an individual family member, I write Scripture prayers as well as practical prayers I'm praying for that child daily. I often record the date beside specific requests. Later I add the day and the way God answered. This has taught me much about God's perfect timing.

During one period I was praying for a daughter away from home who needed a new apartment with lots of storage space. I brought that before the Lord and daily thanked Him that He would provide her with lots of closet space. When he did, I wrote,

"Thank You, Lord," and scratched that petition.

Here are some entries from my prayer journal over the years:

Heal Her Broken Heart
Lord, our daughter's heart is broken. Please comfort her. It was her first touch of love, and now he's dumped her for another girl. Her pride is wounded. She feels rejected, worth nothing. Oh, Lord may she realize how much You love her and we love her. Heal her hurts. Bring other Christian friends into her life who can help fill the void left after losing her special friend. Help her get her priorities in order and realize her real purpose in life should be to love and please You. Thank You for Your everlasting arms around our daughter—Your daughter.

Help Her Accept Herself
Lord, our daughter is almost two heads taller than the other girls in her class. She feels like a giant. Show her You made her just like she is for a purpose. You know what You have in store for her, not only in her physical makeup but with the abilities You have given her. She's struggling hard right now to find her true identity. Please help her see she is special and unique, just as each of Your children is.

Help Me Be an Encourager
Lord, he's not doing as well in school as I'd like. Help me accept his pace. Though I'd like better grades, keep me from pushing him beyond his capacity. Show me how to encourage him, right where he is.

Accomplish Your Will
Today accomplish Your will in my children's lives, Father. Have mercy on them according to Your lovingkindness.

Son's Specific Talent
For my son, who is a graphic artist, I wrote: "May Keith be filled with the Spirit of God, with skill, ability and knowledge in all kinds of crafts—to make artistic designs and to engage in all kinds of artistic craftsmanship" (see Ex. 35:31-33).

Wisdom and Discernment

Lord, give my children wisdom about what they are to look at and listen to. Help them avoid those things that would defile their minds (1 Peter 1:13-16).

Lord, let my children hate this rock music that is so attractive to them now when they are in their teens. May they have a desire to hear music restful for their souls.

Answer:

Some ten years later when I was Christmas shopping with my oldest she was so repelled by the loud rock music, she said to the store manager, "Will you please turn your music down or off if you want me to stay and shop here."

Inside I was praising God for answered prayer. Soft, soothing music is her choice nowadays.

Sample Prayer Journal Page

Child's Name _____

```
┌──────────────┐
│              │
│    PASTE      │
│              │
│    PHOTO      │
│              │
│   OF CHILD    │
│              │
│    HERE       │
│              │
└──────────────┘
```

Thank You, Lord, that You know
the plans You have for
to prosper and not harm him/her,
but to give him/her hope and a future.
I pray that my child will not stand in the
way of sinners or sit in the seat of mockers.
May my child's delight be in the law of the Lord
as he meditates on it day and night
(see Jer. 29:11; Ps. 1:1, 2).

Dear Father, may _____, like Your Son Jesus, grow in wisdom and stature, and in favor with You and the people his/her life touches. Give him/her a listening ear to parental instructions. Help him/her to pay attention that he/she may gain understanding (see Luke 2:52; Prov. 4:1).

May the Spirit of the Lord rest upon my child, _____, the Spirit of wisdom, understanding, counsel, might, knowledge and the reverential and obedient fear of the Lord (see Isa. 11:2, AMP). I pray the eyes of his/her heart may be enlightened in order that he/she may know You better. I pray that

Christ may dwell in his/her heart through faith and that will be rooted and established in love (see Eph. 1:17, 3:17).

How will you begin praying for your child today? Why not write out your prayers as these parents have done?[11, 12]

....

1. Stormie Omartian, *The Power of a Praying Parent* (Eugene, Ore.: Harvest House, 1995) pp. 18-19.
2. Cheri Fuller, *When Mothers Pray* (Sisters, Ore.: Multnomah Publications, 1997), p. 123.
3. Fuller, p. 124.
4. Kent and Barbara Hughes, *Common Sense Parenting* © 1995, p. 91. Used by permission of Tyndale House Publishers, Inc. Wheaton, IL. All rights reserved.
5. Fuller, pp. 129-30, adapted.
6. David and Heather Kopp, *Praying the Bible for Your Children* (Colorado Springs: WaterBrook Press, 1998), p. 15, adapted.
7. Kopp, pp. 15-18, adapted.
8. Quin Sherrer and Ruthanne Garlock, *The Spiritual Warrior's Prayer Guide* (Ann Arbor, Mich.: Servant Publications, 1992), p. 156. Used by permission.
9. Omartian, pp. 13-14.
10. Kopp, pp. 161, 166.
11. Sherrer and Garlock, selections from chapter 2.
12. Gary J. Oliver and H. Norman Wright, *Helping Your Child Become More Like Jesus* (Ventura, Calif.: Regal Books, 1999), adapted from chapter on prayer.

CHAPTER TWELVE

Bringing Your Child Back

Forgiveness and Restoration

Any parent who has a prodigal child longs to bring that child back into the fold, both literally and figuratively. Unfortunately, this is not usually within the parents' power. There are, however, some things that parents can do and say that make it easier for the prodigal child to make the decision to come back—whether he is literally gone from the home, or whether he is only "gone" from the family's values and desires.

When a child is living the prodigal lifestyle, what does she need to hear from her parents? There are some healthy, well-balanced statements that can be made in almost every situation. And the value of these statements is not based on what *you* think of your child; nor is the value based on her response. Don't give your child that much power! She doesn't have to believe or trust or agree with what you say. In your heart and mind, give her permission *not* to agree, and you will take pressure off yourself.

What Your Prodigal Needs

First, *your child needs to know that the door of your house is never completely closed.* Regardless of what he's done, where he's been, or who he is now, he needs to know he can make contact with you again. He may sense this. He may know it intuitively. But it may need to be said or written by you again and again, even if you receive a sarcastic rejection of your message.

In the story of the prodigal in Luke 15, the young man knew that his father treated people fairly. This helped him, not only to *want* to come home, but to have the *courage* to come home.

Sometimes a prodigal is afraid of the response she will receive if she reaches out and tries to reestablish a relationship. One family knew their daughter would be hesitant to reach out to them after being away for three years, living a lifestyle she knew they objected to. When they heard from others that she was interested in reaching out, they reached out to her with a letter that addressed what they felt her concerns might be. This is how a portion of the letter went:

Perhaps you've thought about having a relationship with us sometime again. So have we. Sometimes fear keeps one from reaching out. Perhaps you've had some fears.

You might be afraid that we will judge and condemn you by our words or looks.

You might be afraid that we would say we can have a relationship, but it will never be a good one.

You might be afraid that we expect you to admit that you were wrong and we were right.

You might be afraid that our expectations of you will be so high that you nor anyone else could meet them.

You might be afraid that we will hover over you and try to confine or restrict you.

You might be afraid that we will require you to be involved with us at church.

We just wanted to let you know that *none of these* will happen. You don't have to have these fears. If you have others that we haven't addressed please feel free to bring them to our attention if you so desire. The door to our home and heart is always open.

Second, if there has been an offense against you, *your child needs to know that you desire to forgive.* This could be costly on your part, since you may be dealing with a multitude of broken promises or vows. It could also be costly since true forgiveness means slapping a gag order on whatever it was that was done. It cannot be brought up again in a blaming, accusatory way—nor is the offending party to be reminded of it ever again. But before you let her know you forgive her, you need to understand what forgiveness entails.

As humans, one of our problems is that most of us have a better memory than God does. We cling to our hurts and nurse them, which causes us to experience difficulty with others. When we refuse to forgive God or ourselves (or anyone else, for that matter), we actually play God. When we don't forgive, it fractures, not only our relationship with the child, but our relationship with God as well.

Lewis Smedes asked these questions:

Is it fair to be stuck to a painful past? Is it fair to be walloped again and again by the same old hurt? Vengeance is having a videotape planted in your soul that cannot be turned off. It plays the painful scene over and over again inside your mind. It hooks you into its instant replays. And each time it replays, you feel the clap of pain again. Is it fair?

Forgiving turns off the videotape of pained memory. Forgiving sets you free. Forgiving is the only way to stop the cycle of unfair pain turning in your memory.[1]

Can you accept your child for who he is, for what he may have done, and for what he said to you? This means forgiving to the point where you no longer allow what has occurred in the past to influence you. Only by doing this can you be free—free to develop yourself, to experience life, to communicate in a new way, free to love yourself and your child.

Is it more difficult to forgive friends, business associates, or our family members? Most have said family. It's as though, once we see a child as guilty, it's not written across his name in erasable pencil, but rather tattooed into his skin. When a child rebels, we often give him a life sentence in our mind. Even if he comes back, some parents never let loose of the offense. It lingers. It's on call twenty-four hours a day, ready to be resurrected if there's any hint of the child going off again.

Do you know why we struggle with forgiving our child? We see what she did as a reflection on us. It was either our personality, what we did, didn't do, said or didn't say, our genes, or something else about us that caused her to do what she did. And if *she* were capable of doing this, who else might be capable? That's right. Us!

Our child is an extension of us, and it's as though he turned around and bit us. We could expect this of someone else, but not our own flesh and blood.

When we forgive, we give up one of the tools that may have worked well for us before. Guilt! Now we have to abandon it. We may not have much experience in either giving or receiving forgiveness. It's difficult and awkward.

Forgiveness is an undeserved gift—the gift of releasing.[2]

Remember the words of Dr. Lloyd Ogilvie:

> Who's your burden? Whom do you carry emotionally, in memory, or in conscience? Who causes you difficult reactions of guilt, fear, frustrations, or anger? That person belongs to God. He's carrying him or her too, you know! Isn't it about time to take the load off, face the unresolved dynamics of the relationship and forgive and forget?[3]

Perhaps Webster's definition of the word *forget* can give you some insight into the attitude and response you can choose. *Forget* means "to lose the remembrance of . . . to treat with inattention or disregard . . . to disregard intentionally; overlook; cease remembering or noticing . . . to fail to become mindful at the proper time." Is there a child in your life who is suffering from emotional malnutrition because of resentment and unforgiveness on your part? Could he benefit from your forgetting what he has done?

Not forgiving means inflicting inner torment upon ourselves. When we reinforce those parental messages, we make ourselves miserable and ineffective. Forgiveness is saying, "It is all right, it is over. I no longer resent you nor see you as an enemy. I love you, even if you cannot love me back."

When you forgive someone for hurting you, you perform spiritual surgery inside your soul; you cut away the wrong that was done to you so that you can see your "enemy" through the magic eyes that can heal your soul. Detach that person from the hurt and let it go, the way children open their hands and let a trapped butterfly go free.

Then invite that person back into your mind, fresh, as if a piece of history between you had been erased, its grip on your memory broken.[4]

We are able to forgive because God has forgiven us. He has given us a beautiful model of forgiveness. Allowing God's forgiveness to permeate our lives and renew us is the first step toward wholeness. You want to come to the place where you can wish your child well in all areas of her life, *regardless!*

In forgiving your child, you have the opportunity to practice the grace of God. The outcome, though, may not be what you hoped for, as this parent discovered:

Our daughter has left home four times now. Last week, she called me at work and asked me to meet at a coffeehouse to talk. She told me she was sorry for how she treated us and realized that having a family was important. She said she needed to get out of the relationship with her boyfriend. She said she didn't want to be with him anymore as he was mean to her and was a jerk. She admitted several things had not gone well for her. We often prayed that God would put her in a position where the world would not satisfy her but would make the only door open to be toward God. She, however, was not repentant toward God. This is VERY SIGNIFICANT. We felt maybe we could get her to that place after showing her grace and removing her from this relationship and bad experience. Perhaps this is where we erred. This is after she had been away from home for over one year. There had been very few encounters with her at all, and all of them negative. We told her we would pray about it, relented and helped her move home—even though this was the fourth time. We asked our son how he felt first and we had to ask our youth pastor to talk with him on this as well. Our son was angry toward her. We prayed for a softening of the heart. Our son told us that she would not stay but take advantage of us. We gave her two rules: Go to church with us once a week (she could choose the service) and respect the family. We helped her move home on a Friday. She was sick all weekend, conveniently sick on Sunday. She wanted to go get her mail. My wife told her this was a bad idea as she had just been through so much and would only confuse her. She didn't listen but went anyway. She came back on Sunday night and told me she wanted to move back with her boyfriend. She said she still wasn't happy. She knew we were disappointed because we didn't raise her that way but she didn't believe all we believed. She professed that she still loved God and prayed, but didn't believe that she was doing anything wrong. We talked for an hour and a half, and asked her to at least sleep on it. . . . She got up the next morning and told us she was moving back with her boyfriend. We pleaded with her to think about it and give it some time first. She admitted her friends told her not to go back with him. She said he made her happy some of the time and bought her lots of things. My wife asked her if it was worth losing out on the family again. Our daughter said it was. So we have lost her again. I did manage to ask her to let us salvage some things from the weekend. She has opened her telephone lines to receiving calls from us and we told her we loved her before she left.

Grace costs, doesn't it?

You could end up being hurt or disappointed again. That's the risk of forgiveness.

Stephen Bly puts it this way:

There is easy forgiveness . . . and there is difficult forgiveness. The more serious the offense committed, the more difficult it is to forgive. The less repentant the offender, the more difficult the act of forgiveness. Therefore, if an adult child commits a horrendous crime and shows no remorse or repentance, it becomes a difficult situation for parents. Sometimes both the seriousness of the offense and the sincerity of the repentance are hard to evaluate. Moms and dads may look at things differently and not be able to understand how the other can or cannot forgive the child.

It would be good for both Mom and Dad to chart the seriousness of the offense (with one being minor and nine being major) against the amount of repentance seen (with one being sincere repentance and nine being no repentance at all) and then discuss the other's position before deciding how they should handle a situation with their adult child.

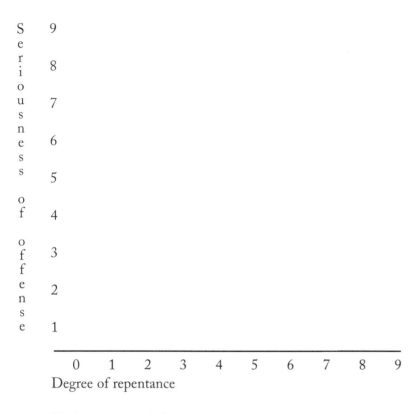

Seriousness of offense

9
8
7
6
5
4
3
2
1

0 1 2 3 4 5 6 7 8 9

Degree of repentance

Truly repentant children, no matter what the acts committed, need your forgiveness almost as much as they need God's forgiveness. And true confession of sin (that is, repentance that leads to a change in behavior) is always accepted by God.[5]

Third, *your child needs to see open expressions of compassion.* The best example of this is the father in Luke 15. This is how Ken Gire describes the scene:

One late afternoon as the father is studying that horizon, a dot suddenly punctuates it. He squints (his eyes are not what they used to be), and the dot becomes more distinct. He follows it down the sloping road until at last he recognizes the familiar stride. It's wearier than he remembers, but it's the stride of his son! And a rush of emotion sends him running.

As the father draws near, he sees a haggard vestige of the person who left home so long ago. The son is unkempt, faint from hunger, and his spindly legs barely support him. But with what little strength he has, he rehearses his scripted confession one more time.

When the father finally reaches him, he doesn't make him grovel in the dirt. He doesn't question him to make sure he's learned his lesson. And he doesn't lecture him: "Look at you, you're a disgrace" . . . "I knew when the money ran out that you'd come crawling back" . . . "You can come home, but only on one condition."

The father says none of those things.

Instead he throws his arms around the son's neck and showers him with kisses, tears rushing from his eyes in a riptide of emotion. The son tries to recite his carefully worded confession, but the father hears none of it. It's not important.

It is enough that his son is alive and that he has come home.

For the son's lost dignity, the father bestows on him a robe of honor. For his bare servant's feet, he puts on them the sandals of a son. For the hand that squandered an entire inheritance, he gives a signet ring that reinstates the son's position of authority in the family business. For his empty stomach, he hosts a feast fit for a king.

A robe, a pair of sandals, a ring, a feast. Symbols not only of forgiveness but of restoration. Gifts of grace, lavished on the one who deserved them least.[6]

Don't Give Up

We as parents face a multitude of temptations in responding to our children. These are easy reactions to fall into, but please avoid them. *Avoid giving up on your children.* You may feel like doing this. Don't. You may have already done this. Undo it. Don't despair. In the midst of anger, resentment, sorrow, confusion, pain, frustration, hurt, fear, helplessness, and anxiety—don't give up. Through these feelings, through it all, keep your focus on the Lord and His grace. You never know when a change can occur. She may need to hear from you that you will never give up on her, no matter what! It could be she has given up on herself. Someone needs to continue to see the value, the worth, the unused and undeveloped potential within her. Write her. Call her. Tell her. Somehow, let her know you haven't lost heart.

Avoid cutting off all contact. Your hurt and anger might be such that you feel as though you can't handle the pain and disappointment any more, so you would rather have him out of your life. It's true you can shut him out physically, but you can't shut him out mentally. Your heart and mind will still have contact. Your children need to know you're accessible. They need to know you exist. Rejection is not the answer; it only leads to further complications.

David shut off his son Absalom. Remember the story?

Then the king said to Joab, "Behold now, I grant this; go bring back the young man Absalom." And Joab fell to the ground on his face, and did obeisance, and thanked the king. And Joab said, "Today your servant knows that I have found favor in your sight, my lord, king, in that the king has performed the request of his servant." So Joab arose, went to Geshur, and brought Absalom to Jerusalem. And the king said, "Let him go to his own house, and let him not see my face." So Absalom went to his own house, and did not see the king's face. Absalom dwelt two full years in Jerusalem, and did not see the king's face. (2 Sam. 14:21-24, 28, AMP)

David *partially* accepted his son back. It's easy to do that. With one hand we offer to receive the prodigal, but with the other we reject and punish. Imagine being invited back to the city where your father lives, but being unable to see him face-to-face for all that time. No wonder he rebelled against David later on.

Even as you receive your child back, however, there are a couple of things to avoid.

Avoid watering down the seriousness of what she did. You can't let her off the hook. You can't participate with her in blaming other people, the environment, circumstances, peer pressure, stress, etc. Often, finding the right thing to say is the hardest step. Rubbing a child's nose in what she's done is not what I'm suggesting. But at some point, it's helpful and healthy for the child to consider and answer the following questions:

What was the purpose of what I did?

Whose lives did this impact and how?

What was wrong about what I did?

What did I learn from what I did?

What will I do differently the next time?

It may be difficult to even consider asking these questions, but they are designed to help the teen or adult child grapple with the seriousness of her behavior, make some value judgments, and then, hopefully, plan for a different response in the future.

Avoid thinking you can do a rescue intervention and make right what was made wrong. There will be some situations your teen or adult child gets himself into that you cannot fix, no matter what you do. Some sins have lasting consequences.

Consider the prodigal son. He may have come home and sought forgiveness, but he had still spent a huge amount of money that was his inheritance. It was gone forever. He could only watch his brother enjoy his portion of the inheritance someday.

He also had to live with knowing he had disappointed his family members, as well as his friends. He came home with a reputation that could haunt him for years. A reputation is one of the most difficult things to ever change. Perhaps he, like so many others, wished he could rewrite history. But that doesn't happen.[7]

Bringing Your Child Home

With these things in mind, the first step in receiving your child back home is *forgiveness.* Forgiveness is a process. Restoring a relationship is also a process, just like healing is a process. It's not an event. It will take time and patience, and it may often feel as though you're taking small steps forward, only to turn around and take giant leaps backward.

Nevertheless, when you do begin to reconcile and rebuild, you want to do it in such a way that the child feels there's an open door that won't be slammed shut, no matter what's discussed.

Regardless of who takes the first step to rebuild, you and your child may both have mixed feelings. It's not uncommon to want to draw closer, but at the same time feel threatened. You may have to fight a desire for avoidance. The timing for how fast the rebuilding occurs varies with each family.

Once the process is started, above all, listen. Listen with your ears, your eyes, and your heart. When your child is talking, don't think about what you'll say when he stops. Proverbs 18:13 says, "He who answers a matter before he hears the facts, it is folly and shame to him" (AMP).

James 1:19 calls us to "be a ready listener." You may not always like what you hear or how it's expressed, but you're not called to be a judge, only a listener. We parents have all used "communication stoppers" over the years. These stoppers intimidate our children or even throttle the expression of their feelings and concerns. Stoppers can include clenching the jaw, pacing, glaring, rolling our eyes, fiddling with papers, crying, looking bored or impatient, or making defensive comments. Try to control these nonverbal expressions as you listen to your child.

You see your child as a prodigal, but she may blame you for something as well. If so, listen, listen, and listen. Don't defend or justify. If you find yourself feeling unsafe, or if your anger is beginning to rise, you may need to take a break or a time-out. If your personality is such that you need to think about your response in the privacy of your mind instead of just immediately responding, there is nothing wrong in doing just that. But remind your child that you need to do this so that she doesn't interpret what you're doing as not listening, stalling, or ignoring.

You might be intimidating to your child no matter his age. You're still the parent and he's the child. Sometimes the anger and disappointment he feels toward himself could be directed toward you. He may also see you as having some responsibility for what he did. He may have anticipated an argument or a lecture from you and respond initially as if that's occurring.

Eventually, your model of good listening may rub off. The Book of Proverbs gives us guidelines to follow:

A man who refuses to admit his mistakes can never be successful. But if he confesses and forsakes them, he gets another chance. (Prov. 28:13, TLB)

If you refuse criticism you will end in poverty and disgrace; if you accept criticism you are on the road to fame. (Prov. 13:18, TLB)

It is a badge of honor to accept valid criticism. (Prov. 25:12, TLB)

Perhaps the words of Peter can be your guiding principles as you begin the process of rebuilding:

Most important of all, continue to show deep love for each other, for love makes up for many of your faults. (1 Peter 4:8, TLB)

Your child needs to be seen and heard by you. He may want to fill you in on the details of what has taken place in his life; or he may not. It's his story and his decision to choose what to share. You may be dying to find out who, what, when, with whom, how much, etc. But don't press. There's a greater likelihood that you will hear his story if you build a relationship first, rather than pushing immediately for details. If and when you do hear his story, treat it as a gift. It's information which he's taken a risk to share and it's a window into his world, whether that world is right or wrong. What he shares is only a reporting of his subjective experience of the situation, of course, but it still can help you understand him.

Children return with varying attitudes. Your hope is that they would repent, turn from their lifestyles, develop a close relationship with you and the Lord. Some will.

Others will come saying, essentially, "I've not done that much that's wrong. You've got the problem. You can't accept me for who and what I am and have done. It's up to you to change."

Others may even be abusive in their response. They're full of rage and complaints, and they project the responsibility for what has occurred onto you. If this happens, you need to set some clear boundaries as to what you will accept. If what they are saying is abusive, attacking, and demeaning, then after they've said it once, it doesn't need to be repeated. Whenever your child does share her story, thank her for being willing to trust you enough to share.

If she does put some responsibility back onto you that could be valid, you do need to validate your child's reality. It's not important that you agree with her perceptions. Remember, each of you will have a different memory of the same situation or incident.

Even if you interpret your son or daughter's situation differently, you can still be empathetic and say, "You know, I can understand how it seemed that way to you. I may have felt that way too."

Most parents struggle with guilt and self-blame, as we've said earlier in this book. Even after you've worked through all of that and realize your child has free will and that some of the way he acts is based on genes, you may still wish you had done some things differently. I do. I wish I had known thirty years ago what I know now. I wish I could have responded in ways then that I know how to now. But we're not to live with regrets. It's an energy drain. When there is a regret, express it to your child, no matter what it is. Don't justify, explain, or rationalize whatever you feel you may have done. You're not looking for your child to comfort you; you are looking to take responsibility for your share of his problems.

Your greatest struggle will be to *contain* (not stuff) your feelings during this time. It's as though, once we become a parent, we develop this desire to tell, teach, moralize, straighten out, and correct, and most of this comes from feelings—perhaps anger, bitterness, shame, guilt, hurt, regret. You probably have your own list.

Sometimes you're shocked by what you hear. Sometimes you're hurt. You may feel fear or disappointment. It may take you time to reflect on and process what you've heard. You may need to say, "I guess I need time to think about what you said. I do want to talk further with you about this. I just need to sift through what I've heard and what I'm feeling. Thank you for sharing with me."

You may *not* want to hear or deal with what he is sharing with you. You may become numb, shut down, or feel unresponsive. A parent shared with me that this happened to her when her adult daughter, who had been sexually promiscuous and into drugs for years, said, "You want to know why I did what I did? I'll tell you. I was angry at Dad, the pillar of the community. For years he sexually abused me. I couldn't tell anyone. So I decided to get back at him. He ruined me, so I'd ruin his reputation." If for any reason you begin to shut down, you may need to say, "I'm starting to shut down. Maybe it's fear. I don't know. I'd like to hear you, but I guess I can't right now. I do want to talk, but I need to work on me today."

If you have genuine regrets about something that occurred, the words "I'm sorry" are important. These words *don't* mean you're a bad, evil person, but rather, "I wish I could rewrite that part of the past, but I can't. I am responsible for this and you can count on that not happening again."

Bear in mind that some children will continue to maintain distance in their relationships with their parents. You are not responsible for that. Once again it is their choice.[8]

1. forgiveness
2. reconciliation

The other step in receiving your child back home is **reconciliation**. Unfortunately, some lump forgiveness and reconciliation together. But you can't. They're separate. Forgiveness is unilateral. It's something you do yourself without any participation or response on the part of the other person. It's your choice. It's under your control. Reconciliation, however, goes both ways. One person can't do it. It takes two who are in sync with one another to some degree. Both sides have to want this to happen. Both need to accept their contribution to the problem. They need to know what each other feels about what happened and to have worked through the process of repentance and forgiveness.

In the story of the prodigal, there was reconciliation between the father and the youngest son, but not between the two brothers. The older brother held on to his resentment toward his brother. Not only that, he resented his father for accepting his brother back. The father tried to reconcile with his older son, but it appears the older brother resisted reconciliation with either.[9]

Is it possible for reconciliation to take place between you and your prodigal child? This is what it will take.

- Forgiveness. Forgiveness is nothing that can be earned—it must be given. You can't buy back a relationship. Dave Stoop says, "The beauty of both forgiveness and reconciliation is that they are free actions that come from the heart."[10] You are responsible for forgiving your child, but in order for reconciliation to take place, your child must be willing to forgive you as well.

- Acceptance. For reconciliation to occur, there must also be acceptance. And, like forgiveness, it must be mutual. Acceptance involves several features:

It means both of you have to be able to accept yourselves and each other with your strengths as well as defeats.
It means both of you need to be willing to admit your own failures.
It means both want healing for the broken relationship.
It means both have to be willing to give up their demand that they were right.
It means both have to be willing to give up any desire to make the other pay.[11]

Have you and your prodigal child reached the point where these things are true? I hope so. If not, pray heartily and fervently that the day will come.

....

Lewis B. Smedes, "Forgiveness: The Power to Change the Past" *Christianity Today,* 7 January 1983, p. 26.

William Coleman, *How to Go Home Without Feeling Like a Child* (Dallas: Word Publishing, 1991) pp. 105-6, adapted.

Dr. Lloyd John Ogilvie, *God's Best for My Life* (Eugene, Ore.: Harvest House, 1981) p. 9.

Smedes, p. 37.

Stephen Bly, *Just Because They've Left, Doesn't Mean They're Gone* (Colorado Springs: Focus on the Family, 1993), pp. 111-12.

Ken Gire, *Instructive Moments with the Savior* (Grand Rapids, Mich.: Zondervan Publishing House, 1992), pp. 57-8.

Bly, pp. 109-16, adapted.

Lorie Dwinell and Ruth Baety, *We Did the Best We Could* (Deerfield Beach, Fla.: Health Communications, Inc., 1993), pp. 370-74, adapted.

David Stoop and James Masteller, *Forgiving Our Parents, Forgiving Ourselves* (Ann Arbor, Mich.: Servant Publications, 1991), pp. 264-67, adapted.

10. Stoop and Masteller, p. 268.

11. Stoop and Masteller, pp. 269, adapted.

CHAPTER THIRTEEN

You, Your Family, and Survival

It may seem as though your prodigal has damaged your family beyond all hope of repair. Deep as the damage goes, however, your family can survive.

Survival is a choice. Like so many other issues in life, we do have a choice regarding how to respond to the curveballs our prodigal has thrown us.

If you think that things will never be the same, you may be right. Crisis and change go hand in hand. The question is, do you want to be a victim of the direction this change takes you, or do you want to be in charge of it? Everyone has a choice after a crisis hits. The definition of a survivor is a person (or family) who gets knocked down and stays down for the count . . . then gets up and does things differently. The non-survivor just gets back in the ring and gets hit all over again. That hurts! And when you're dealing with a lingering prodigal issue, there's enough pain already.

If you've already experienced a crisis, you know what I'm saying. Some parents and families draw closer together and become more compassionate. Others become splintered and soon disintegrate. Some individuals stagnate while others grow, even as they carry wounds and scars.

Many families, instead of working out solutions for their pain and problems, begin to attack each other. If conflicts have been buried for years, a crisis lifts the restraints, and conflicts erupt with a new source of fuel. Now your family has to deal not only with the crisis itself, but with other unresolved conflicts as well. Each drains energy needed to cope with the other.

A family works together like a large body. Each person is an integral part of the body. When one part of the body refuses to cooperate with the rest and does its own thing (as a rebellious child does), all the other parts are affected. They have to learn to adjust. Sometimes they must assume new roles.

It's similar to balancing an old-fashioned scale. If something is added to one side, it alters the other side by the same amount in the opposite direction. If the scale is ever to be balanced again, something has to be added to one side or subtracted from the other.

Your family is like that scale. The members have to adjust to handle the change and get back into balance. Many aspects of family life—including power, responsibilities, and roles—may need to be reassigned. The longer the central individual was in the family or the greater the significance of his or her position—if, for instance, the oldest child rebels—the more adjustments will need to be made.

I've seen cases in which one child committed serious offenses that drew attention away from the parents' marriage problems. When the child was jailed and no longer at home, the marriage problems became apparent, and another child became the troublemaker to ease the marital tensions. It works the other way as well. Perhaps the marital problems could be swept under the carpet as long as all was smooth sailing with the children. But when a crisis arose with a child, it drew out all the tension that had been festering between the parents.

Between the time a crisis occurs and the individual family members discover their new roles and begin to stabilize, there's a time of uncertainty and turmoil. Because of the reality of the loss, it's difficult to make some of the necessary changes. Each family member needs time and space to deal with the crisis in his or her own way. It may take a while for each one to find a new role. Each feels like a juggler at times, trying to deal with his or her own needs and still be helpful to the other family members.

After a prodigal crisis hits, you'll also have to weigh the needs of a particular family member against the needs of the family as a whole. You'll have to work to achieve a balance. What do you do, for example, when a child runs away close to Christmas? How do you respond when some of the family members want to get a Christmas tree and celebrate the holiday and some don't?

Tips for Survival

How do people survive a crisis? How do families survive? How will you survive? Must a person have a certain type of background or upbringing to be a survivor when a crisis hits? No. With the right approach, anyone can survive the prodigal experience. The following are characteristics of crisis survivors.

Survivors Choose the Right Attitude

I never expected that my daughter, at the age of twenty, would take a detour from her Christian life and live with boyfriends, use cocaine, and move into alcoholism. But it happened, and it continued for four years.

I never expected to have my only son born profoundly mentally retarded because of brain damage and then suddenly die at the age of twenty-two. But it happened.

Over the years, my wife and I have learned the truth and significance of many passages from God's Word. One passage in particular came alive as we depended on it more and more: "Consider it all joy, my brethren, when you encounter various trials, knowing that the testing [or trying] of your faith produces endurance" (James 1:2-3, NASB).

The Amplified Version goes on to say, "But let endurance and steadfastness and patience have full play and do a thorough work, so that you may be [people] perfectly and fully developed [with no defects], lacking in nothing" (James 1:4).

Learning to put that attitude into practice is a process. The passage does not say "respond this way immediately." You have to feel the pain and grief first, and then you'll be able to consider it all joy.

What does the word *consider* mean? As I studied in commentaries, I discovered that it refers to an internal attitude of the heart or mind that allows the trials and circumstances of life to affect us either adversely or beneficially. Another way James 1:2 might be translated is this: "Make up your mind to regard adversity as something to welcome or be glad about."

You have the power to decide what your attitude will be. You can say about a trial, "That's terrible. Totally upsetting. That's the last thing I wanted for my life. Why did it have to happen now? Why me?"

The other way of "considering" the same difficulty is to say, "It's not what I wanted or expected, but it's here. There are going to be some difficult times, but how can I make the best of them?" Don't ever deny the pain or hurt you might have to go through, but always ask, "What can I learn from it? How can I grow through this? How can I use it for God's glory?"

The verb tense used in the word *consider* indicates a decisiveness of action. It's not an attitude of resignation: "Well, I'll just give up. I'm stuck with this problem. That's the way life is." If you resign yourself, you will sit back and do nothing. But James 1:2 indicates you will have to go *against* your natural inclination to see the trial as a negative. There will be some moments when you'll have to remind yourself, "I think there's a better way of responding to this. Lord, I really want You to help me see it from a different perspective." Then your mind will shift to a more constructive response. This often takes a lot of work on your part. Discovering the truth of the verses in James and many other passages like that one will enable you to develop a biblical perspective on life. And that is the ultimate survival tool.

God created us with both the capacity and the freedom to determine how we respond to the unexpected incidents life brings our way. You wish that a certain event had never occurred, but you can't change the fact that it did. The key word here is *attitude*. You can choose which attitude you will have! Listen to the story of one woman.

The day had started out rotten. I overslept and was late for work. Everything that happened at the office contributed to my nervous frenzy. By the time I reached the bus stop for my homeward trip, my stomach was one big knot.

As usual, the bus was late, and jammed. I had to stand in the aisle. As the lurching vehicle pulled me in all directions, my gloom deepened.

Then I heard a deep voice from up front boom, "Beautiful day, isn't it?" Because of the crowd I could not see that man, but I could hear him as he continued to comment on the spring scenery, calling attention to each approaching landmark. This church. That park. This cemetery. That firehouse. Soon all the passengers were gazing out the windows. The man's enthusiasm was so contagious I found myself smiling for the first time that day.

We reached my stop. Maneuvering toward the door, I got a look at our "guide": a plump figure with a black beard, wearing dark glasses and carrying a thin white cane. Incredible! He was blind!

I stepped off the bus and, suddenly, all my built-up tensions drained away. God in His wisdom had sent a blind man to help me see—to see that though there are times when things go wrong, when all seems dark and dreary, it is still a beautiful world. Humming a tune, I raced up the steps to my apartment. I couldn't wait to greet my husband with "Beautiful day, isn't it?"

—Source Unknown

Survivors Realize That the End Result Is in God's Hands

Those who survive realize that God is in control of the way things turn out. We do all that we can do, but then we rest in Him. As it says in Psalm 37:

Do not fret because of evil men or be envious of those who do wrong;

for like the grass they will soon wither, like green plants they will soon die away.

Trust in the Lord and do good; dwell in the land and enjoy safe pasture.

Delight yourself in the Lord and he will give you the desires of your heart.

Commit your way to the Lord; trust in him and he will do this:

He will make your righteousness shine like the dawn,

the justice of your cause like the noonday sun.

Be still before the Lord and wait patiently for him;

do not fret when men succeed in their evil ways,

when they carry out their wicked schemes.

Refrain from anger and turn from wrath; do not fret—it leads only to evil. (vv. 1-8)

Hillary and Chad have two adopted children, a boy and a girl. Hillary was a teacher at a Christian school when their daughter ran away the first time. After she repeatedly ran away and broke the trust that relationships need to be built on, Hillary and Chad had to make the decision that their daughter could not come back home unless major changes were made in her behavior. At the same time, Chad's business was floundering, due

mainly to his own poor management. Their dreams were crumbling.
Hillary shared how she got through the rough times:

Our issue with our daughter was a matter of trust. That was my
loss—a loss of trust in her. We are still experiencing that loss.
But as I lost trust in her, I began to grow in my trust in the Lord.
The first night she ran away, I came to the realization, "If you
can't trust God when it's three o'clock in the morning and your
thirteen-year-old daughter is missing, when can you trust Him?"
I decided there would never be a better time to start, so I went
to bed and went to sleep. The next morning at six, she called us
and wanted to come home. That was the beginning of her
running and the beginning of my trusting.

Hillary knew she was getting better when she came to the point
where she knew others didn't understand and it didn't matter that they
didn't understand. She knew she was okay with God, and that was all
that mattered. Hillary observed that the problems she and Chad had
with their daughter turned their marriage around.

Having to deal with her made us deal with our own lives and
with our marriage. If we hadn't had to deal with her, I don't
know where we would be today.

The last time their daughter left, she had just turned seventeen.
Hillary and Chad didn't hear from her for three months. At that point
Hillary gave up.

We had done everything we could have done: prayer, searching
Scriptures, making contracts with her, positive affirmation, stern
discipline, gentle discipline, meeting and entertaining her
friends, changing schools, home schooling, counselors, consistent attendance at church and youth group, etc.
    When I gave up, Psalm 131 became my solace. I pictured
myself as a weaned child, one who demands nothing, climbing
on God's lap and sitting there quietly, confident in His love for
me and His ability to handle this situation.[1]

Survivors Learn to Express Their Feelings

In order to survive, you learn to express your feelings—all of them. We talked about this earlier. Survivors find healthy ways to express hurt, anger, bitterness, depression, and resentment. They don't bottle up the feelings, nor do they merely complain. They talk, they write, they share, they pray, and they cry—men and women alike. Bottled up feelings remain alive and interfere with life.

You'll be angry. Oh, will you ever! It's a feeling that mobilizes you into action. Anger is a sign of protest. It's a natural and predictable emotion after a crisis or loss. It's a reaction against something that shouldn't have happened. It's a way of fighting back when you feel helpless. Your perception of the way things are or the way they should be has been altered. Your belief system has been damaged. Anger is a normal reaction when you are deprived of something you value.

Too often, there is no appropriate object on which to vent our anger, so we begin looking for anything! At whom do we get angry most often? God. We blame Him—He shouldn't have done this or He shouldn't have allowed that. He's supposed to do things right, which means according to the way we want it! Why didn't He protect or redirect our child, especially when we prayed for him every day?

When you blame God, it can be unnerving and unsettling to other people. They either respond with Christian clichés, or they try to convince you that your anger at God is irrational. They fail to realize that nothing they say will help, because you are living on emotions at this point. Even though you may be raising questions, you're not really looking for answers.

We also get angry at others who haven't had to experience what we've gone through. Because they haven't experienced, or we think they haven't experienced, the devastation that we have, part of us wants them to have the opportunity. It's especially annoying when they talk about how good or gifted their own child is at this time.

You may get angry at those who fail to reach out and support you during this time of trouble. When we hurt, we want to be acknowledged. We don't want people to pretend that everything is okay, because it isn't. And in some cases, it will never be—at least, not in the way we have always defined "okay." Of course, part of the reason we end up feeling isolated is that few people have been taught how to minister to people during a time of need. Fortunately, this is starting to change.

How do you deal with anger in a positive way? You admit it, you accept it, you release it in a healthy way. You use anger's energy to do something constructive.

Perhaps you could write a letter (don't mail it!) to whomever you're angry at, and then sit in a room and read it aloud. Many people have found release by journaling each day. The point is, those who are resilient come to grips with their anger, and their other feelings, in constructive ways.

A friend of mine, Jessica Shaver, wrote the following poem that depicts what so many people have discovered.

I Told God I Was Angry

I told God I was angry.
I thought He'd be surprised.
I thought I'd kept hostility
quite cleverly disguised.
I told the Lord I hate Him.
I told Him that I hurt.
I told Him that He isn't fair,
He's treated me like dirt.
I told God I was angry
but *I'm* the one surprised.

"What I've known all along,"
He said,
"you've finally realized."
"At last you have admitted
what's really in your heart.
Dishonesty, not anger,
was keeping us apart.
"Even when you hate Me
I don't stop loving you.
Before you can receive
that love
you must confess what's true.
"In telling me the anger
you genuinely feel,
It loses power over you,
permitting you to heal."

I told God I was sorry
and He's forgiven me.
The truth that I was angry
has finally set me free.

Survivors Talk about What's Happening

Over the years, we've found that families who have difficulty coping frequently hurt one another by keeping silent. During a crisis, interaction among family members is vital. Often, however, they retreat into their own inner worlds and don't express their thoughts or feelings. Sometimes some family members want to talk but others don't. The family may not communicate during difficult times because they never learned to talk when everything was going well. People aren't likely to have the energy, time, and capability to learn communication skills when life is falling apart around them.

It may be that another child in the family feels torn between loyalty to her sibling and loyalty to her parents. Or the child feels the anger of the parents and doesn't want it directed at him. Maybe he just has no idea what to say to the sibling who has caused so much turmoil. This child, like all family members, needs the help of others.

It's encouraging to see the number of support groups that have been established in churches throughout the country. A church in northern California has a class on parenting rebellious adolescents during the Sunday School hour as a regular part of its ministry. Another group, this one in Canada, studied a variety of resources, sometimes focusing on prevention, other times on intervention. A unique feature was the development of a negotiating team from the group of parents. This team assisted a young girl return home after she had been away for two months. What helped her respond positively was the fact there were so many caring adults.

One of the problems that will become apparent in any group is that some parents will attend looking for microwave solutions. They want an instant remedy that just isn't available. They usually don't remain in the group, and, unfortunately, they often take steps that create additional problems between themselves and their child.

It's been my observation that parents who either attend a special support group or have a group of friends who function as a support group are able to weather this storm better than those who try to tough it out on their own.

All parents need others who have walked, or are walking, where they are at the present time. They need others who really mean it when they say, "I understand."

Parents—and siblings—need a safe place that comes equipped with the accepting compassion of others in which to dump their feelings and frustrations. Sometimes other families who have a rebellious child have greater insight on what to do for and with your child than you do. You may be low on faith and hope. Others can lend you theirs until yours returns. When you're low on confidence, others can lend you what you need. Other parents will be able to see progress when you're unable to see any.

Survivors Do Not Live Independently

Most people don't realize that a silent person has power over other family members. For those who want to talk, the silence adds to the pressure of the crisis, and they end up feeling rejected and isolated. Survivors learn to draw on their own strengths and gifts and use them effectively, yet they still ask for and can accept assistance from others. They can also express concern and warmth to others. Silence is a characteristic of dysfunctional families; it destroys and deadens hope. And as the silence progresses, estrangement and frustration increase. If a person doesn't know what to say, begin with that statement. It's a contribution. **Don't allow one family member's silence to isolate the rest of you.**

Survivors Focus on Solutions, Not Blame

Families who survive and grow concentrate more on solutions than on blame. Blame is one of the most significant characteristics of individuals and families who *don't* make it during difficult times. No one likes being out of control and left hanging. We yearn for some closure, to discover what created the problem in the first place. If we have an explanation for what happened, we can understand it better, handle it better, and feel relieved that someone else was at fault. The more serious the crisis, the greater the need we feel to discover the cause. Statements that start with the words, "If only you had/hadn't . . ." or "Why didn't you/Why did you . . ." begin to fly between one person and another. If a family member knows the other person's areas of vulnerability, the accusations can get vicious.

You may not want to blame others. But blame directs the attention away from you. You know that blaming doesn't make sense. But good sense doesn't often prevail after a crisis. Rather, the surge of emotional turmoil and the struggle for a reason for the difficulty becomes uppermost. When you blame, you create a war zone and the other side retaliates.

Because everyone is vulnerable at this time, accusations and other comments penetrate deep into the mind and heart of the one on the receiving end. They will be remembered for years. No one wants to be unfairly accused or blamed.

In the Book of Proverbs, we read, "There are those who speak rashly, like the piercing of a sword" (12:18, AMP) and "In a multitude of words transgression is not lacking" (10:19, AMP). These verses clearly reflect the pain of unfair accusation.

It's a difficult temptation to resist. But blaming only makes the problem worse.

Survivors Don't Magnify the Problem

Families who do not cope well often magnify the seriousness of their problems. They take them to the extreme and imagine the worst possible consequences, instead of being hopeful or waiting to see what the actual results will be. They interact too much and in the wrong direction. When they discuss their crises only among themselves, without outside objective assistance, they easily become pessimistic. They're not solution-oriented but problem-centered. They often use the "victim phrases" that reflect a desire to just give up:

"I can't . . ."
"That's a problem."
"I'll never . . ."
"That's awful!"
"Why is life this way?"
"If only . . ."
"Life is a big struggle."
"What will I do?"

These kinds of statements take a problem from bad to worse. And sometimes, they can be a self-fulfilling prophecy. Rose-colored glasses may not be helpful, but magnifying glasses can be just as detrimental.

Survivors Don't Become Bitter

Bitterness will try to creep in when prodigal behavior begins, but survivors shut the door in its face. They refuse to live in the past or permit a situation to stop them in their tracks with no hope for the future. Bitterness comes from focusing on the unfairness of whatever has happened. It's like a warplane's radar locking onto a target. Bitterness leads to resentment, and the bitter person becomes a victim.

Sometimes in discussing a painful situation, you hear someone say, "Don't tell me to forgive her! I'm not about to. She doesn't deserve it!"

The natural response of anger and resentment causes pain, to be sure. But too often we choose to let it stay in our lives and gain a foothold. This is another time to write an unmailed letter, either to the person causing the crisis, or even to the crisis itself, odd as that may sound. Write as much as you can under the headings "I resent . . ." and "I wish . . ." In time, your bitterness will lift, and that's the first step toward forgiveness.

A similar problem that will keep a person and the entire family stuck in the past is an attitude of resignation: "I give up. Why try? She won't change. This will always be a problem. The other kids will probably turn out that way too." You believe you're defeated already, so you don't give God much room to work in the crisis or in your heart. There were times when I wondered about our daughter, "How long will this go on? It's been three years already!" But it's important to keep your eyes on your hopes for the future, not the bitterness of the past.

Survivors Want to Learn and Grow

Survivors aren't people who merely make it through the crisis. They are people who overcome the crisis—who come out on the other side better and more mature than they were before.

In the Book of Revelation, we find statements to the churches that are being judged. Each time, there are words of great hope and encouragement given to "him who overcomes." It is to the overcomers that the Lord makes these promises (NASB, emphasis added):

To him who *overcomes*, I will grant to eat from the tree of life, which is in the Paradise of God. (2:7)

He who *overcomes* shall not be hurt by the second death. (2:11)

To him who *overcomes* I will give some of the hidden manna, and I will give him a white stone, and a new name written on the stone which no one knows but he who receives it. (2:17)

And he who *overcomes*, and he who keeps my deeds until the end, to him I will give authority over the nations . . . and I will give him the morning star. (2:26-28)

He who *overcomes* shall thus be clothed in white garments; and I will not erase his name from the book of life, and I will confess his name before my Father, and before His angels. (3:5)

He who *overcomes*, I will make him a pillar in the temple of my God, and he will not go out from it anymore; and I will write upon him the name of my God, and the name of the city of my God, the new Jerusalem, which comes down out of heaven from my God, and my new name. (3:12)

He who *overcomes*, I will grant to him to sit with me on my throne, as I also overcame and sat down with my Father on His throne. (3:21)

To learn and grow means you must reach out to others, admit what is going on, and ask for help. And it will be there for you in abundance, for God never turns His back on those who reach out to Him.

Survivors Find Comfort in the Scriptures

Holding on to the truth of Scripture and its promises helps individuals and families get through the difficult times. God said, "Be strong and courageous! Do not tremble or be dismayed, for the Lord your God is with you wherever you go" (Josh. 1:9, NASB). He also promised, "For I know the plans that I have for you . . . plans for welfare and not for calamity to give you a future and a hope" (Jer. 29:11, NASB). The Bible is full of such comforting and motivating passages. Find them, study them, cling to them.

Survivors Put Fears Aside and Forge Ahead

When there are unresolved conflicts within a family, it's easy to say, "Why even bother?" when it comes to relating. Many families simply give up trying to listen to or engage others in conversation. A healthy family overrides its fears and discovers ways to make things better. Members learn to solve problems and are willing to listen to one another and try something new. This approach is a source of encouragement and hope in the midst of heartache.

It's also important to determine which problems are worth tackling, which are not, and which ones can be resolved. At times, you'll need to postpone problem-solving or take a break from it.

Successful families believe that each person has the ability to handle adversity. They don't suffocate one another with words like "You should . . ." or "You ought to . . ." Instead of being overbearing with advice, they encourage one another. Unconditional love is the backbone for their relationships.

Survivors Respect Their Differences

Each member of the family is likely to cope with the crisis in a different way. One may need to take action—to read books about prodigals, look into treatment facilities, meet with every support group in sight. Another may get more comfort from prayer and quiet walks; another may need to put it out of his mind, occupying his time and thoughts with anything but the problem. The families who cope most successfully with a crisis are those who respect each other's personality differences. If a person needs to talk or do something—or needs privacy and quiet—that's all right.

Maybe these characteristics are not all in place in your family. That's all right. But they are good goals to work on, ones that will not only help you cope with this crisis, but will make your family stronger and better afterward as well.

In our survey, we asked parents to share things they did that helped them survive their prodigal experience. Perhaps their answers will help you as well.

> Turned to the Lord, spouse, godly friends, and professionals for counsel. For some time it really did feel like mere survival. The pain was so great and the grieving so deep there were days I did not function well. . . . (Coming to the place where I could even believe all that happened took me time.)

> For my survival I joined a parent support group at our church called "Parenting Within Reason" and purchased Buddy Scott's book *Relief for Hurting Parents*. Others in the group understood my pain. To have someone to relate to was a great help.

> How did I go on with my life? I stayed in the Word daily. I regularly was attending church. I admit I was weak. I cried a lot and was obsessed over my lost daughter. I'm so powerless over her actions. I thank the Lord for those of faith who continually prayed for my daughter and my family.

> I didn't do anything for survival. I just existed by doing all the little mundane things like getting out of bed or brushing my teeth.

> I went on with my life with a new realization. I thought I was a godly servant only to find out that I was an ungodly, codependent doormat. With this realization came action in the areas of counseling, reading, and Christian group help to start anew.

We went for counseling and took our daughter for counseling as well. We joined a parent support group. We learned to just try to make sure that she knew we loved her.

After we kicked her out, the increase in peace in the home and decrease in stress was immediately noticeable.

The best thing we did was join the parent support group. They were using Buddy Scott's book. That book and the support were awesome.

The first thing we did was call some very close friends over—at 2 A.M.—and cried and prayed with them. We then shared it through some tears with our Sunday School class who was very supportive and still is. I felt we needed to have others praying and I didn't think keeping it quiet would allow for the body of Christ to apply prayer—it would only be those whom we told—therefore we had to get it out. It also opened doors for others to tell us that they, too, were living with the same thing. In some cases, they didn't tell others, and in other cases they had talked freely about it.

Our daughter ran away three times before the permanent move out to live with her boyfriend. Each time we allowed her back. We set up a family mission statement and rules for the house when she came back and asked her to agree to them before staying. We joined a prodigal cell group at our church. We had previously bonded with a family that also was experiencing the same problems. We agreed to pray daily for each other's daughter and to be there for each other. My wife and I were in total agreement in how we would respond to our prodigal daughter, how we would not enable her lifestyle in sin, and we worked hard to fix the relationship with our remaining son. We encouraged his Christian walk and were concerned at this point that she would influence him negatively as well. My wife started fasting each Thursday and prayed each day for our daughter. I joined her a few months later and we are still devoted to fasting and praying for our daughter.

The most important thing we did was PRAY.

I sought prayer support, counsel from one of our church pastors, spoke with Barbara Johnson, head of Spatula Ministries, on the phone and read (more like devoured) her book *Where Does a Mother Go to Resign?* I felt like I needed to know someone who had been raised like me—in a solid Christian home—and had raised her child much the way I had with solid Christian teaching from both parents.

I went on with my life by staying as busy as I could. I rearranged furniture and the bedrooms in the house—we bought a new couch and even a new car!

After suffering silently for what seemed like forever, we finally sought help. Our son had gotten himself in trouble with the law so that was kind of the breaking point for my husband, so he sought help through Child and Family Services. They assigned us a worker who spent a lot of time talking with us. The stages one goes through are similar to death, the isolation so painful that just to have someone who understood and offered suggestions really helped me. She suggested a parenting support group she was starting called "Parenting Toward Solutions," which focused on finding positive small steps. This helped me so much to work through some things in a small group setting. . . . I found when problems kept occurring it was so easy to only see the negative. In our local community paper at the same time, an ad appeared advertising for a parenting group at a neighborhood Baptist church called "Parenting Within Reason." It was based on a book written by a U.S. author, Buddy Scott, called *Relief for Hurting Parents.* We joined this weekly group, which met for an hour of teaching and then an hour of support groups. My husband and I are still a part of this group. Through this group we have come to realize that so much is out of our control in terms of our son; however, our reactions, attitudes, etc., are in our control. We are learning to take control over our emotions better. I believe if you were to ask Adam he would tell you we are better parents than we were a year ago. The tools we have learned have helped us in parenting our other two teens as well.

At first I was paralyzed, I tried to talk with a friend or two who found it hard to listen to my pain. I was given Scripture (e.g., Rom. 8:28) and patted on the back with a "you'll be okay." I felt very alone. I didn't need to hear Romans 8:28; I knew all of that. I needed to be validated, loved, and accepted. My husband was there for me and allowed me to work through it. It was hard for him to hear my pain, he had his also. God was the one I ran to; I told Him everything, the good and the bad. I expressed anger to Him for allowing [our daughter] to go her way. I never felt shamed by God for expressing my anger. He kept His arms open wide for me to come just as I was. I went on with life by keeping busy with our other children, got involved with Bible studies, volunteering, and some part-time work.

[We] made sure we had time to get away together and talk. (Had "dates" at least once a week). Thanks to the availability of my parents we were able to get away together for occasional week-ends and one time for a one-week cruise. There were times we used the time "away" to listen to one another's pain and work on the next move and other times we would agree to "have fun" and not mention one thing about our prodigal. There were times we needed to get away from it all and remember our love and commitment to one another. During one of the times of getting away (Valentine's) we went to the motel we had gone on our honeymoon (even the same room) and we made a list of ten things we appreciated about one another. It was healing and affirming during a time we felt otherwise unloved and unvalued.

Read books on the subject.

Began a support group at our church of other <u>P</u>arents <u>of</u> <u>Teens</u> (we call ourselves the "Cracked POTS"). We have used Buddy Scott's book *Help for Hurting Parents* as our textbook.

Began (for me) and kept up with (my husband) an exercise program.

Joined a weight loss group and took off twenty-five unwanted pounds.

Redecorated house and specifically my daughter's room (which became her brother's room).

Went through photo albums and was reminded that we really did have some good times.

Wrote, framed, and presented tributes to my parents. Seeing life from a new perspective gave me new appreciation of my parents. It was healing and beneficial to express those thoughts to them. (It was read, by the way, in front of all our children, including my daughter, at Christmastime).

Began a journal where I wrote one thing I was thankful for each day.

Read the Psalms and Job in *The Message*.

Sought out an older Christian woman and met weekly for prayer and mentoring.

These ideas may help you, or you may find other things more helpful. But whatever you do, find *something* that works. You can survive. Life can be good again. But it's up to you to make it happen.

....

1. Marilyn Heavilin, *When Dreams Die* (Nashville: Thomas Nelson Publishers), pp. 36-37.

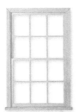

CHAPTER FOURTEEN

Learning from Other Parents

In this chapter, I'd like to invite you into the lives of other parents of prodigals. They didn't want to experience what they have been through. It hasn't been easy. The pain of their journey will be obvious. But they are willing to share their stories in order to help you, and others like you. Their stories take the form of answers to three questions on a survey.

The first question was this: "What new insights did you gain from this experience?"
Every painful experience of life brings the opportunity for growth. Here are some of the things these parents learned.

It was brought home how much I hurt God when I disobey.

Man certainly has free will. There are hurting parents all over. One person's actions affect the whole family. Life doesn't get easier.

Would I do anything differently than I did? You bet I would—knowing what I know now. But I didn't know it when I made the decisions in the past and I can't reclaim them. I made those decisions then to the best of my ability. I tried not to be selfish, though at times I'm sure I messed up on some things here too. The real point is we *cannot change the past*. We must move on with principles that help us deal with it now.

It has been my observation, and in some cases, experience, that when the powers of sex, drugs, food, and alcohol begin to take control of your life, you must mount an attack against these. You can't just walk away from them. You must walk *towards Christ* with your whole being. Every thought must be brought into captivity for the sake of Christ. Every friend must contribute to your growth and survival or he or she must be abandoned (at least until you are strong, which may mean for a long, long time). My son didn't do this. He kept walking back into the arena of sin, which only strengthened his desire for it.

Sure, as parents, we make mistakes, but we didn't teach our child to deceive us, to lie to us, to seek sin. We did the best we could; it just wasn't enough without his making the same commitments we made.

Faith—God is faithful.
Hope—There is always light after the tunnel of darkness.
Love—Love overcomes all. God's love is so strong and powerful. He'll never let go of us.

For adopted children to experience rejection is not uncommon. They in turn can choose to reject their adoptive parents' faith or lifestyle for no logical reason. In searching for meaning in this situation, I began to see the comparison between being adopted into God's family and yet having the freedom to choose to reject God's plan for our life and go our own willful way. Although I did not make a practice of sinning, there were areas of worry and times of doubting God's control that were not Christ-like responses. Christians all have problems and having a prodigal was our opportunity to trust God for His deliverance from the far country.

Well, I know I am far less likely to judge other people's actions when they have a child who walks away from the Lord. Before I used to look at the parents and say, "Well, they must have done something wrong!" I've also learned to absolutely lean on the Lord for my strength to get through some days. I don't understand why or how this happened, but I know God is still in control and I will trust Him to work in my son's life and draw him back where he belongs. I also think I have a different outlook on homosexuals, in that now I see them as someone else's children who may be putting their moms and dads through the same pain we're going through.

The Lord provided help for our daughter-in-law through me. She, being a very loyal oldest daughter, couldn't complain about her husband to anyone who didn't love him as much as she did. That was to me, his mother. The Lord gave me a special dispensation. I was able to listen to the things she was going through with him and sympathize with her as though we were talking about a stranger, rather than my son. The problem with that for me was switching back to think of him as a son in a "normal" way.

The person with the prodigal needs to remember than when that person promises to change he really thinks he is going to. We seem to be highly insulted when the prodigal "lies" to us, but it helps to realize that at the time he makes those promises he fully intends to keep them. In other words, he is really lying to themselves rather than to us.

A. I don't always have to be right—but I need to be well, healthy, loving and whole. It's never too late to start doing (or learning) what is right; e.g., how to communicate better with my children.
B. Pride will hold me back and make me appear that I am without need. Pain has been the gateway to a humbleness that's making me more approachable.
C. It's not what's happening *TO* me but what's happening *IN* me that is important.
D. I have had a deeper awareness of who God is and a clearer picture of who I am (my great sinfulness and need for a Savior). I experienced anew God's grace, which, I have learned, must not only be accepted but also extended to others.
E. If I am to stand for righteousness there will be suffering. Suffering is painful and may even be inflicted by those we love the very most. I have had to ask myself, "Am I willing to suffer (to be misunderstood, ridiculed, unforgiven, etc.) for Jesus? The answer is yes!
F. God can, will, and desires to meet all my needs.
G. Life is brief and precious. I must live each day that God gives to me

to the fullest by honoring Him in all I do.

H. My children are God's children; we are in this thing together. I was given custody, not control. I was never guaranteed anything. I must not take all the credit when things go well and neither do I need to take all the blame when things don't go well. When my children were babies I had a false sense of control. I have never had control over my kids; God does. I can't control my teen's choices but I can choose my response. I can become bitter and unforgiving, filled with resentment, or I can trust God. God can and will guide if I ask. I can respond with His power and love.

I. My attitude "should be the same as that of Christ Jesus . . . who . . . made himself nothing, taking the very nature of a servant, he humbled himself and become obedient to death—even death on a cross. . . ." (Phil. 2:5-8)

J. Never say never. Satan is alive and well and today's youth is being bombarded with more evil and lies than any age group in the history of the Western nations. I thought there were kids who were well prepared to face the pressure and wouldn't be deceived. Now I know, if my daughter could be so deceived it could happen to anyone.

This has made us really think about things that we "put" on our children. We knew that it was difficult for our children to be the PKs (pastor's kids); to always be judged by a different set of rules than other children and young people in the church. Though many in the church tried to judge and criticize the behavior of the children of the ministry (a group of about six kids), we tried to allow our daughter the freedom to be who God created her to be, at the same time setting boundaries that would guide and shape her.

None of our friends back home in the church where our daughter did her growing up could ever imagine that our daughter would be the one of that group of pastor's kids to ever stand up to the fishbowl and say, "No more, not me," but she did. So we are taking another look at that fishbowl, and trying to diffuse any future crisis with foresight rather than hindsight.

Now that some time has passed (nearly two years), I have had some in-depth conversations with my prodigal. One day I asked her point-blank "WHY" she had left. I told her I didn't want to pry, but I also didn't want to make the same mistakes with the other three kids, and wanted to try to understand. She still did not have much of an answer for me, except to say that now she knows it wasn't because of us, but it was something she had to do. At the time she was angry at us and felt that she had missed out on life because of her life as a PK. She also said that she knew the Lord was pinpointing areas in her life at the time, and she chose to run from the confrontation rather than listen with her heart and allow Him to bring direction and correction. She was searching for who she was, and was afraid she'd never know if she stayed. Our daughter knows that the way she left was wrong. That it brought pain on herself as well as her family. But she also knows that she had to make the journey one way or another. There were other ways to do it, but she knows that she had come to the place where she had to allow God to deal with her. Finding herself in God was the true test of this prodigal trip, and the price for that is beyond measure.

To others who are suffering the same loss, we would say don't ever give up on God. His mercies are new every morning, and His grace is sufficient for all we need.

Physically, I have faced death and come out with a renewed zeal to move ahead. Dealing with a prodigal is different. It has brought seemingly unending grief into my life. I'm not sure I have the emotional strength to survive. But if I truly believe any part of Scripture, I have to believe Jeremiah 29:11, which tells me, "For I know the plans I have for you, plans to prosper you and not to harm you, plans to give you hope and a future." If this is true, God has a plan that I am unaware of . . . a plan that will give me hope and a future. I am learning to trust Him a little more each day. And if this promise is for me, it is also for my daughter. I long for the day when her relationship will be restored to our Father in heaven.

The issues of blended/stepfamilies is complex. Two families trying to parent is especially difficult. Providing a united front is so important for a teen, and it has been especially difficult for them and for us with two families trying to parent a child. When those two families are giving conflicting value messages, is it any wonder that kids today are confused? When I (the natural mom) and stepdad say, "I love you enough to provide boundaries and expectations," and the natural dad and stepmom say, "I love you enough to let you do whatever you want within reason," there is confusion. What is within reason? Most teens would like the option of not having to face the consequences for their poor choices, and unfortunately, teens with more than one "home" have that option. In a nuclear family such an option normally does not exist. If there is not a relative who is willing to take the child for awhile, family members are forced to face one another, reconcile, and learn how to get along. Is it any wonder that children from broken families don't know how to have healthy relationships?

We had a real positive experience meeting with two other couples anywhere from two times a month to once every two months. We poured out our hearts and prayed for each other and could trust each other's confidentiality. We learned we didn't have it as bad as others. It was an outlet and made us realize even more that others are going through similar crises. We used Ruth Graham's book *Prodigals and Those Who Love Them*. She helped us to look at God and ourselves and how we will relate to Him versus what we can do to change our prodigal. It was a book that ministered to me.

The second question was this: "What practical advice would you give to others?"
May the wisdom they gained through hard experience minister to you.

A. PRAY. Don't think, "Now all I have left to do is pray"; rather, know that prayer is the most powerful and productive thing you can do. You have a most awesome privilege and your child has a great advantage over other prodigals who don't have praying Christian parents.
B. Don't orchestrate their rescue. Let them learn by their own mistakes and let the road of hard knocks show them the reality you have been trying to tell them about.
C. Love them with unconditional love. Continue to let them know you love them no matter what. You may not love what they are doing, but let them know you will never stop loving them.
D. Learn how to let go. This was something I didn't know how to do.
E. Understand you are in the midst of a grieving process and let yourself go through it. Let other people help you. Use this time for your own personal growth. This is a time for great change in your own life. (I feel I have learned so much at my daughter's expense and I'm sorry she had to pay such a high price for my learning).
F. Keep the door open. Be ready whenever they are ready to "come home." Become a place (person) of safety, not judgment and condemnation.

G. Be available and create opportunities to get together but respect their lack of interest and response; e.g., "Would love to meet you for lunch between classes, just let me know when the time is right for you." After a few invitations with no response, drop it and respect their need for distance at this time.

H. Keep a sense of humor. Get a good joke book or start reading the funnies and cut them out and put them on the refrigerator so you can remember to laugh at least once a day.

Keep loving them; pray for them and yourself. Make sure you are right with God. Find Christians who will support you in word and deed. Keep the lines of communication open. Pick your battles wisely. Depending on the situation, don't push or try to force them to change, but maintain reasonable boundaries. If they have physically left home, keep the physical and emotional door open. Don't lose hope. If they are still living at home and are minors, get a reality check from other Christians regarding the boundaries you have set and stay with the reasonable ones. Be willing to change your boundaries, but not your principles. Pray, pray, and pray.

KEEP THE LINES OF COMMUNICATION OPEN! One of our pastors gave us this advice and we are so glad we took it. He explained that some parents have reacted so strongly that the communication is broken forever. We always told her we love her and are there for her. Things continue to get better.

Number 1—Find a support group, preferably one with a Christian leaning. Get [a go-between] for those times when your prodigal comes calling, especially if he or she demands things, etc.

Number 2—If you have other children, support them and love them. They are probably hurting as well.

Number 3—If the prodigal phones, love him, but if he is demanding, tell him that he has to talk to (put name of go-between here).

Remember other times when you had a difficult struggle and saw the Lord's hand helping you through it. Remember those times when He helped you when you didn't ask for His help in prayer, or you didn't recognize it until after you were through the struggle looking back. You begin to see that God looks out for you because He loves you, not because you can analyze the situation and then specify what you need in prayer and He then supplies. He is working even before you ask, even before you think to ask, because He loves you, cares for you and wants the best for your life.

When you understand that God is at work to achieve the best in your life, you will begin to see that He is at work to achieve the best in your son or daughter's life. When you retain control you become part of the problem, not part of the solution.

Your son or daughter has chosen to go his or her way; it can be fatal—and this hurts. But your best chance of changing that choice is to let God do the work and you come alongside with a willing spirit ready to do what He directs in your child's life—not what you want.

Ten Tips for Survival

1. Play worship songs and offer to God the sacrifice of praise (Hab. 3:17-19)
2. Search the Scriptures according to James 1:25. Meditate on the Psalms of David, who cried out to the Lord for mercy and grace in his times of distress.
3. Ask God to give you the patience to endure suffering (James 5:10-11).
4. Pray for your prodigal without ceasing (1 Thes. 5:17).
5. Take every thought captive and refuse to think the worst about the consequences of the sin (2 Cor. 10:5).
6. Make a list of all the attributes you are grateful to God for putting into the life of your prodigal (Phil. 4:8).
7. Confess your sins and regrets to a prayer partner and ask that he or she agree with you for restoration (James 5:16).
8. Look for the rainbow in the midst of the storm (Gen. 50:20). Never forget that God is ALMIGHTY.
9. Frequent your local Christian bookstore section on recovery and grief. There are some basic tools to help you through the stages of grief once you realize this is similar to a death. There is comfort in knowing you are not alone in this experience and neither are you losing your mind.
10. Having done all, "STAND" (Eph. 6:13). Refuse to give in to self-pity or to run from God, blaming Him. Believe that God's perfect love is greater than your human love and memorize 1 Corinthians 13, until you begin to use this as your nightly prayer to help when sleep won't come.

A. Be consistent. Stay steady. Believe in the power of consistent prayer and fasting. Sometimes it seems the prodigals want to watch and see if your faith is really what you say it is. Even though you have professed it for years, walked through valleys, and not given up, it doesn't appear they got the message that you REALLY mean it.

B. Don't give in to enabling your kids and their sinful lifestyles. Don't weaken because of wanting to keep a relationship. My mother did that—did anything to keep a relationship with a bisexual daughter in a horrible lifestyle, including condoning all she did. Mom thought this would allow her to keep channels open and witness to my sister. Nothing in twenty-five years has happened except that my sister feels that she is perfectly okay and continues on her merry way in total darkness. I know this does not work.

C. Don't allow people to force you to change your actions. The worst advice often comes from the people you love and respect, which makes it twice as hard—your relatives and some well-meaning, but misinformed, Christians.

I guess my advice would be to be as open as possible with family and friends and enlist their prayer support for everyone involved. Don't ostracize your child—let her know you love her for the real person inside—but don't condone what she is doing. Let her know you want her to keep in touch and let the Lord show you places where you can reach out and say, "I love you." The last thing I would say is to pray for your child continuously and realize that you can't force your child to pick up your values, standards, faith, etc.; she has to make that choice for herself. You just have to be faithful to teach and train her what God's Word says.

1. Do not blame—ourselves, spouses, child, or his or her friends. Admit the situation.

2. Do not be overly fearful and emotionally blow the situation out of proportion. We need to first deal with and clear away all our emotions—fear, control, shame—and not allow Satan to discourage and play on our imagination.

3. Seek help—attend workshops and talk to parents with past experiences. Get emotional and spiritual support from church.

4. Pray and trust God is in control and He will help us.

5. Love our children unconditionally (not how they behave). Until we're emotionally strong and healthy we won't be able to listen to their

needs. Do not overreact by pushing them away. They'll seek love and support elsewhere—from friends who cannot help them.

6. Trust that *they still love us* and *need us*. Look beyond all immediate situations.
7. Recognize it's a phase and many others also went through this—maybe in a different form.
8. Seek *good* Christian counseling for good communications.
9. Do *not compare* our family and children with others. Do not feel sorry for ourselves.
10. Look to the Bible for truth—we're all sinners and God is there to save, forgive, love, and heal, and to protect us from the Evil One.

Ask God to send someone who will come alongside you who will listen without giving advice, will support you, validate you, and allow you to bleed all over her and still love and accept you and have confidence in you. Be sure to not stuff your pain. Run from those who try to fix you, shame you, tell you the mistakes you made, use Scripture that makes for guilty feelings, don't have time to listen, condemn you, tell you it will be okay but that you have to forgive (you know that and will work through to that point in time). After you have worked through it and are experiencing peace that God knows all the details and will work in it, trust His sovereignty and get busy helping others. We got into a small group, "Parents of Prodigals."

If you are waiting—be patient, trusting the Lord to work. I've been praying some of the spiritual warfare prayers in the pamphlet by Ted Haggard titled *How to Take Authority Over Your Mind, Home, Business, and Country.*

The third question was, "What would you tell parents *not* to do?"

Parents, don't put your son or daughter's value down as a person. Don't describe them negatively or attack them with vulgar or curse words. Don't slap them or gossip about them or compare or show a lack of confidence in them to do better.

Do not lose hope. If you've been a Christian for a long time and raised your family in the church, they know the right path to take. They must make their own choices. If you are a new Christian, they will see the changes in your life. It may take some time, but again, they must make their own choices.

Don't put off things that will (hopefully) force the prodigal to reflect on the differences between the home and the pigs. Don't procrastinate on getting help.

Don't ignore the problem, hoping it will go away. Don't worry about what the neighbors/friends/relatives will say. If your rebel is apprehended by the authorities, don't defend him, let the system teach him. Follow Buddy Scott's advice and get a complete physical for your rebel (if he is available).

Do not create a barrier that your children cannot cross back over to come home again. For now they are out there, somewhere, doing their thing, but because it is sin, it will crash in around them; if they know Christ, the Holy Spirit is still working on them. When it crashes in, you want them to come home for support, for love, and help back to a normal life.

I would tell other parents not to be vindictive. It's so easy to seek revenge when your child has hurt you so much. Ask God to help you forgive your child. Don't cut off any channel of communication. Don't turn your back on your child, don't blame yourselves for the choices your child is making, don't bear this burden all alone, but be open with as many people as possible for support, and don't fail to pray faithfully for your child to return.

Don't take things personally. Yes, it's so easy to say and so hard to do. Our job suddenly becomes to "be a wall." We are the ones he/she needs to bounce things off of and see what happens. He/she needs us to be strong, convicted, and directed, yet real, honest, open, and vulnerable. At this time, however, I was confused, hurt, angry, and felt abused, unloved, and unvalued. Try to be the adult and realize that he/she is working so hard to be independent from you that he/she can see very little from your eyes.

Don't work overtime always having the perfect answer and rebuttal. Listen to hear his/her perspective rather than always giving yours. Share your own pains and struggles as a teen (if you can remember back that far!). Be real and vulnerable, not necessarily one who has all the right answers.

When our children go wrong we are angry and hurt. The last thing we would think of doing is throwing a party. Wouldn't that just condone what that "stupid kid" has done? Yet that's exactly what God does for us. He's throwing a giant party for us. It's called eternal life. We enter through the doorway of forgiveness from all our sins. (Every evil thing that Prodigal Son of the Bible had done was left outside the door of his father's house when he finally returned home). But growth and healing take time—in our lives and in the lives of our children. Sometimes God interjects a miracle. But more often than not, He works through circumstances and other people to help both our children and us to grow and mature.

"The healing process is not always what we think it should be," write Dave and Jan Stoop, who struggled for years with a wayward son. They continue:

> There is something much deeper going on, that we sometimes catch a glimpse of, that transcends our need for an immediate solution to a pressing problem. It's so easy to get caught up in a system, even a system of faith, that guarantees specific results. In our efforts to put into practice the principles of trusting, committing and resting, we found ourselves stepping into the area of presumption because we lost sight of who was in charge. . . .
> We desperately struggled with our "system" of faith. Sitting at coffee with a friend one day, at the darkest point of our struggle, he pressed us for an answer to the question of where God's sovereignty fit into our "system." In our search for a miracle, we lost sight of the object of our faith—God, Himself. As we reaffirmed our trust in His sovereignty, we discovered the miracle was already taking place. The miracle was taking place—*within us!*[1]

A miracle can take place within you too. Trust God to make it happen.

....

1.   Dave and Jan Stoop, *A Parent's Cry for Help* (Eugene, Ore.: Harvest House, 1981), p. 127.

CHAPTER FIFTEEN

You, Too, Have a Choice

What Will It Be?

A s a couple, we came to the conclusion that our role was to pray and attempt to love Sheryl unconditionally. Joyce recalls her thoughts and concerns at that time:

"My friend Fran and I felt led to pray and ask God to confront Sheryl and get her attention. We began daily to put her in God's hands, and we prayed that He would use whatever means necessary to bring her back to Himself. Sometimes God uses dramatic and painful events to draw us back. We discovered a pattern occurring after we prayed. In two or three days she would call—needy, hurting, and frightened over some incident.

"Through the years of concern, Norm and I were able to sleep at night, even though we knew her chosen path could lead her into a great deal of trouble. We prayed for her protection and released her into God's hands.

"A particular incident stands out in my mind. We were out of town, conducting a marriage seminar in the Grand Teton National Park. One night I awakened with a burden for Sheryl and just knew she had a great need at that time. All I could do was pray, knowing God knew what that need was. When we returned home, I casually mentioned to Sheryl what happened, and she asked about the day and time of my concern. When I told her, she thought for a moment, then turned very quiet and pale, inwardly recalling where she had been at that time. It was a moment when she realized that God still loved her and was trying to reach her.

"We can remember other times when Christian women were able to sit and talk with Sheryl while she did their nails. (She's a manicurist.) Who will ever know how much Sheryl was influenced by others during that time? Keep praying for the recovery of your children and a spiritual healing in their lives."

Here are three things you may need to remind yourself *not* to do: Don't pry, don't preach, and don't pressure a young adult who is either wandering or has returned.

After about three and a half years, we began to see indications of change in Sheryl's life. A friend asked her to accompany her to an Alcoholics Anonymous meeting for moral support. To Sheryl's surprise, as she heard the testimonies and information, she realized, *They're talking about me. I need to be here too.* We never thought that one day we would be sitting in an AA meeting, listening to our daughter stand up and say, "Hi. My name is Sheryl. I'm an alcoholic"—and then watch her receive her thirty-day sobriety pin. But we've seen her conquer that problem.

A few months later, she had to enter the hospital for an operation on a herniated disk. While she was there, she told Joyce, "I just hope and pray that God will let me live through this so I can turn my life around and find my way back to Him."

A short while later, a Christian man who is married to one of my relatives was visiting. As he talked with Sheryl, he asked her, "What are you going to do with your life?" That really set her to thinking.

That same weekend, we all went to church together at the First Presbyterian Church of Hollywood. Our pastor, Dr. Lloyd Ogilvie, was gone that Sunday, and Ralph Osborne was preaching. At the conclusion of services, there is an opportunity for people to come forward to invite Jesus into their lives, to recommit their lives to the Lord, to receive prayer for healing, and so on. I will never forget sitting in the silence of that moment and then hearing a quiet voice in my ear say, "Daddy, will you walk up there with me?"

With tears in my eyes, I followed her to the front of the church and had the privilege of seeing her kneel there, talk with an elder, and then recommit her life to Jesus Christ. It was a commitment that included a dramatic turnaround in her total lifestyle.

Later that day, Sheryl said, "Daddy, I was doing fine emotionally until I looked at you and saw that you were losing it, and then I lost control and cried too." We both laughed at her comment, realizing we were crying tears of joy. Joyce and I are so thankful that God can turn years of heartache with our children into occasions for great joy. Because of the dramatic change in her life, her female roommate became violent, and Sheryl had to move back home. But two days later her girlfriend accepted the Lord, and the next day they led her brother to the Lord, and several years later, her own father accepted the Lord and turned his life around dramatically.

You may not be there yet. Your child may still be wandering. It may seem like forever. And for some, it could be. Sometimes parents won't see the wandering child return. But never, never give up hope. Keep praying. And perhaps for you, as it happened for us, the Parable of the Prodigal Son in Luke 15 will take on more significance. Actually, we can all relate to that story, because in one way or another, aren't we all prodigals? It's just that some of us are more obvious than others.

Let me conclude on a positive note as a means of encouragement. The joyful occasions that you thought you'd never see *can* become a reality.

I've been talking about the shattering of our dreams for our children. There's nothing wrong with dreams—as long as they are realistic and have not been set in concrete. We naturally want our children to be a reflection of our beliefs, values, and standards.

I had high hopes for our daughter's academic success. I now understand the reasons for my expectations much better than I did then. When I realized my retarded son, Matthew, would never progress much beyond a two-year-old mentally, my hopes for Sheryl and her academic pursuits increased dramatically. I *assumed* she would attend and complete college. After all, since I had completed college and two graduate programs, why wouldn't Sheryl follow that same path?

But those were my dreams, not hers. Sheryl quit college after one year and became a licensed manicurist in a nail salon. Her career choice wasn't what I would have chosen, but I was not the one to choose. And then she began to excel in her field. She applied her God-given artistic talent to her work by doing nail art—painting miniature scenes on the nails of her customers.

Sheryl learned most of what she did on her own, without benefit of lessons. She would create a new idea and never stop to think it couldn't be accomplished. She also learned the art of air brushing on her own and even designed some new nail styles. Her skill developed to the point that she has won almost all of the national competitions in this field, taught for a major nail company, and opened her own nail salon, in which she did her own interior decorating.

She has developed her own line of products and now teaches internationally. But more important than anything is the ministry she has with women who come to her to have their nails done. Some have failing marriages, some are having affairs, while others are involved with substance abuse. Most of them wouldn't share with a pastor or counselor what they share with Sheryl. And she's able to tell them of her own journey and her Lord who is able to change their lives as her life was changed.

This was one of the reasons for writing this book. My wife and I have walked the path you are on. We, too, had the choice to focus on the pain and disappointment—or to let the pain cause us to grow and change for the better.

What are you learning about yourself, your faith, the mercies of God, and handling the hurts of life?

You, too, have a choice. What will it be?

It might be helpful for you to hear the story of what one mother has experienced. It's an ongoing journey for it's not yet complete. It encompasses many of the elements and topics addressed in this book. You will probably identify with this experience, perhaps learn from it, and, I hope be encouraged by what is said:

"We have been married twenty-eight years. My husband is and has been an emergency department RN for over twenty years. I have a background in nursing and medical social work. I currently am in my second year of elementary teaching. Nursing plus erratic hours has been a source of family stress to us. We have a son, twenty-four, who is well adjusted and happily married. He is more temperamentally like my husband and myself (quiet and cautious); he was relatively easy to raise even during his teen years. We raised him from a young age to be responsible and accountable for his choices; he is/was a cautious child and he weighed his decisions before acting. We tried raising our daughter the same way, but it has been a very different experience. Our daughter, seventeen, has always been an 'in your face' child: demanding her own way, demanding attention, very impulsive; she looks at the moment and doesn't want to think about possible consequences; she is a major 'control' person. These tendencies became more pronounced during her teen years. My husband I tend to be peacemaker/negotiator types. It has been extremely difficult to guide her because she doesn't want to hear anything that conflicts with her own opinion. To give a balanced picture, our daughter has a compassionate heart and is a loyal friend; she is a gifted musician and athlete; she is quite artistic. We raised both our children in a church environment and we have tried to role-model and discuss biblical values in our home.

"Our daughter was diagnosed with ADHD at the age of twelve (largely through my reading and initiating medical/psych contact in this regard). She was on Cylert from ages eleven to fifteen. She was weaned off it by a new doctor and seemed to do satisfactorily off it. Towards the end of her tenth-grade year (the Crisis Year) she was diagnosed with ODD (oppositional defiant disorder). I was told this was learned behavior and not very changeable. I have come to believe that super-strong will, impulsivity, and failure to regard consequences is not learned but inborn. That super-strong will has a positive side; it all depends on how it's channeled.

"Everything was a big issue to her—definitely worth fighting for. We felt in a catch-22: she was showing us that she wasn't responsible to make many decisions, yet she pushed against us unmercifully to have control over her life; she also lied to us and blamed virtually all her problems on parents, teachers, classmates, etc. She also already had more freedom than we were comfortable with. No matter what we did she wanted more.

"The key issues we had to deal with were poor impulse control, deception, and other manipulative behavior plus lack of willingness to be involved with family. At the age of fifteen and a half she became sexually involved with a long-term male friend from church (sixteen years old). When we suspected this intimacy and tried to discuss it with her she completely denied it while at the same time she was telling her adult brother that she thought she might be pregnant. After they broke up, she threatened to take an overdose. We got her into grief counseling, which helped her work through her acute suicidal ideas. Several months after the breakup, she and a girlfriend allowed three adult males from out of town to pick them up. They were taken to a remote park where a forest ranger found them all drinking in the back of the van. My husband and I and the other girl's parents discussed the seriousness of the situation with the girls on several occasions. We supervised them even more closely; we tried to point out the strengths and talents of both girls. (This friendship was long-standing and though they didn't always make good music together we just prayed and tried to supervise. We decided not to force their separation, relocate her to another school, or move out of town because we felt that our daughter would 'find her element' wherever she was; also, we felt she might rebel even more so. She was sometimes the initiator also.) These situations, after years of low-grade but chronic stress in our relationship, were the ultimate stressors. We were extremely concerned for her physical and emotional well-being.

"During this Crisis Year, my husband and I discussed everything openly and decided that we would not allow these traumas to destroy us. In the past sometimes he felt I wasn't strict enough but I requested he interfere more frequently with her directly on issues instead of through me. This helped him understand what I was dealing with; he became more empathetic. I continued in the Parents of Teens support group though it was months later before I felt able to discuss these issues with the group. The prayer support from the POTS group was helpful. Sharing with a close friend who had been a prodigal teen was also helpful. Up until that time my attempts at getting counseling to improve our communication had met with canned and misguided programs. My husband and I attempted to continue with our other responsibilities in life plus we tried to spend more time doing hobbies, social activities, time together, etc., so we could maintain some perspective. We tried to stay focused on present issues. We tried to focus on solutions and not blame. We worked hard at communicating clearly. I, in the past, would often rise to the bait as she frequently baited me unmercifully into arguments. I started going for walks at times of potential verbal explosions; I refused to take her places or even be in close quarters with her if she was in an argumentative mood. My husband and I agreed that when she pressured me for a decision and would not accept my input that I would refer her to her father. Whenever we planned activities with our daughter she would habitually stage a major 'bait and fight' with me shortly before our time together. For a while I simply stopped asking for family time. I envisioned the future without her wanting to be part of the family. I used 'thought stopping,' a cognitive therapy technique whereby each time I caught my self 'fortune telling' a dismal future I would simply tell myself to 'stop it'; then I would paint a mental picture of a happy future for all of us together. I tried to encourage her to dream dreams and create goals. She would have nothing to do with dreams and goals. I backed off, said little, and spent my time trying to make myself feel good about what I had control over. I cannot change her; it's difficult enough to change myself. I would like to say that there was a miraculous turnaround with these changes. What made the biggest change, though, was when we were finally able to get her to see a woman psychiatrist who had a good reputation for doing well with teenage girls. Jane had always refused to see a counselor either on her own or with us previously. However, she was so miserable this Crisis Year that she finally asked to see a counselor. (In addition, she was also flunking out of school and getting into verbal altercations at school). The psychiatrist stated she didn't normally believe in prescribing medication for teens. After reading our extensive history and spending a session with our daughter she put her on a small dose of Wellbrutin (an antidepressant) right away. Gradually over the next two weeks we saw a major difference. Our daughter said she didn't really feel much different but the psychiatrist said that this was not unusual. Within less than two weeks we were having meaningful conversations together; even when we disagreed we could do so usually in a much more reasonable manner.

"We continued to try to let our daughter know we loved her. We tried to focus on the positive. Sometimes we succeeded, sometimes we felt like giving up. We continued our lifelong prayers for her and our family. (This Crisis Year was definitely a time of spiritual despair for both my husband and myself.) We continued to hold her accountable for her choices; when we thought she was lying we would tactfully address this issue (often then she would confess).

"My husband and I are learning to let go of the self-blame and the blame that society puts on parents. I have a greater sense of humility and compassion towards other parents with challenging children. I have come to see that our job as parents is to love unconditionally, yet be able to establish boundaries that we are relatively comfortable with (quite a juggling act). I have a greater gut level feeling of what it must be like for Christ to continually love wayward humanity.

"I have come to realize that she felt she wasn't getting the attention she needed. (In reality she got a tremendous amount.) What I've learned though is that I need to acknowledge her feelings and feed her feelings back to her but NOT rush in with how she could have prevented something or do it better. At the same time, we need to hold her strictly accountable for contracts we set up with her. I also need to limit the discussion surrounding a situation. My tendency is to negotiate and EXPLAIN my reasons for my decisions. This opened the door to arguments as my reasons were rarely 'good enough' for her. I now tell her 'I'm not comfortable with that but, in time, you'll have more opportunities.'

"The story is not over; she has been seeing this psychiatrist for only six weeks. We are more hopeful than we've been in years, though. My hope, my dream, is that she can explore anger management, determine her values and goals, dream dreams that will become reality. We have had to adjust our expectations, we are trying to love her as Christ would love her. (I felt like I was accepting her for her but she felt like she had to measure up to some preconceived perfect child, she says). Christ doesn't care if she has tattoos and body piercings. Christ won't love her any less if she chooses to take her GED and/or chooses to forgo college. She needs to feel we love her regardless of her choices. Now that she's calmer she can see and hear that we want to love her—not her choices. Christ knows that she chose to be baptized, that she has a loving heart. I feel deep in my heart that the storms we have been through with her will help us and her relate to others."

Your journey may not be over. Your life has been changed and will continue to be changed by this experience. God can and will use this experience for your growth and His glory. Remember this even when it's hard to believe. And when you hit the depth of despair and wonder if your child will always be running away from God, remember the words of Psalm 139, first from *The Living Bible* and then a paraphrase by Larry Crabb.

O Lord, you have examined my heart and know everything about me. You know when I sit or stand. When far away you know my every thought. You chart the path ahead of me, and tell me where to stop and rest. Every moment, you know where I am. You know what I am going to say even before I say it. You both precede and follow me, and place your hand of blessing on my head.

This is too glorious, too wonderful to believe! I can *never* be lost to your Spirit . . . if I go down to the place of the dead, you are there. If I ride the morning winds to the farthest oceans, even there your hand will guide me, your strength will support me. If I try to hide in the darkness, the night becomes light around me. For even darkness cannot hide from God; to you the night shines as bright as day. Darkness and light are both alike to you. (vv. 1-12)

Fleeing from You
Fleeing from You,
nothing he sees
of Your preceding
as he flees.

Choosing his own path
how could he know
Your hand directs
where he shall go.

Thinking he's free,
"free at last,"
unaware that Your hand
holds him fast.

Poor prodigal!
seeking a "where" from
"whence,"
how does one escape
Omnipotence?

Waiting for darkness
to hide in night,
not knowing, with You
dark is as light.

Based on Psalm 139:7–12
in light of Luke 15.[1]

....

1. Larry Crabb, *Connecting* (Nashville: Word Publishing, 1997), p. 38.